Taking the Mystique out of Learning Disabilities

A Practical Guide for Literacy Tutors

Ricki Goldstein

Laubach Literacy of Canada
Copyright 2000

Table of Contents

Introduction   4

Defining Terms   6

The Rich and the Famous   14

Identifying Adults with Learning Disabilities   18

How Learning Disabilities Affect Adults   25

Diagnosis   28

Identifying Specific Problems and
Determining Educational Needs   30

More about Remediation   41

Attention and Concentration   47

Irlen Syndrome   51

Technology and Learning Disabilities   54

Compensatory Strategies   61

Accommodations   65

Studies, Surveys and Statistics   68

The Devil's Advocate   78

Conclusion   79

Recommendations for Literacy Providers   81

Bibliography   84

Appendices   86

Foreword

As the Executive Director of a literacy council called RECLAIM (the Reading Council for Literacy Advance in Montreal), I had long felt the need to learn more about learning disabilities. With the increase in publicity about literacy, more and more students who have learning disabilities were coming forward and asking for help. Yet there was a mystique about this category of students. Even experienced tutors were apt to say, "Don't give me a student with learning disabilities. I don't know anything about that kind of problem." This guide is intended for literacy tutors, practitioners, students and anyone who, like me, has the desire to know more about learning disabilities.

My first step was to find out more about learning disabilities than I had learned in my teacher training. I arranged two workshops on the subject for our tutors. These were conducted by Dr. Margie Golick, a psychologist now at the Learning Associates of Montreal. For over 50 years, Dr. Golick and her colleagues have specialized in evaluating and teaching students with learning disabilities, and in research into the nature of those difficulties. The workshops taught us a great deal, and certainly took away the mystery. They taught us that there are no esoteric teaching techniques, just good teaching principles. Although learning disabilities are constitutional problems—part of the individual—and are generally permanent, the best approach is to figure out what each student needs to know, and how he can learn it most effectively.

All of us who participated in the workshops gained more confidence in our own teaching efforts. We sharpened our abilities to recognize these students, learned to figure out their strengths and weaknesses, and added several techniques to our teaching repertoires. Over the years, I continued to work in the area of learning disabilities. I read, attended conferences, gave workshops on the subject, and continued to observe literacy students whose problems stemmed from learning disabilities. I also consulted in the area, developing curriculum materials such as tapes and books for students, tutors and teachers. Having worked on projects for Laubach Literacy of Canada, the Quebec Ministry of Education, the National Literacy Secretariat, and the Learning Disabilities Association of Canada, and having worked with Dr. Margie Golick, I gained a great deal of insight and knowledge about the subject.

In this guide, I hope to pass along information I have learned in workshops, through reading, through consultations with Dr. Golick, and through my own experiences as an educational consultant, literacy teacher and Executive Director of a literacy council. I hope that you will learn something new, but I also hope that you will recognize that the most important aspect of teaching students with learning disabilities is what you have been doing all along: encouraging your student, being patient and caring, giving generously of your time, and above all, meeting your student's needs.

I would like to take this opportunity to offer my sincere thanks to Dr. Margie Golick for all her help along the way, and for the guidance and encouragement she has so generously given me when consulting on this book.

Introduction

Over the years, I have had the great pleasure to meet and work with several outstanding literacy students whose problems stemmed from learning disabilities, and I have shared many joyful moments with them as they shone in a variety of situations.

Desirée was the first to intrigue me. She had graduated university but still needed reading and writing remediation to help her with work-related tasks. Today Desirée speaks candidly about her learning disabilities, is a certified family life educator, and has been on RECLAIM's Board of Directors.

Cheryl, a successful factory forewoman and a determined RECLAIM student, made incredible gains. She took her tutoring seriously, sought a professional learning disabilities evaluation from which she learned a great deal, and ultimately enrolled in a junior college. All this contributed to Cheryl's markedly increased self-esteem.

Pesha, termed a "dumb" student when she was young, was later thrilled to learn that she only had learning disabilities. In fact, Pesha is an extremely articulate, bright and creative individual, who became a professional writer. She now speaks publicly about her literacy problems and learning disabilities, but with enthusiasm and pride. Among her accomplishments, Pesha recently published a collection of humorous and heartfelt writings called *Chicken Soup*.

As a tutor, you have the opportunity to help a student with learning disabilities achieve full educational potential. Working to the best of your ability, you will make a difference in a student's life. Obviously, it is too late now for "early" diagnosis, but certainly some diagnostic techniques, corresponding remediation, compensatory strategies and accommodations in classes, teaching sessions or on the job will make a difference to the literacy student whose problems stem from learning disabilities.

I commend you on your interest in learning disabilities, your awareness that not all literacy students are alike, and your grasp of the notion that this very special group needs special attention and treatment.

You may note that I have avoided using the term "learning disabled", and have used the sometimes awkward term "...with learning disabilities". I have done so because the original term "children with learning disabilities", coined in the 1960s by Samuel Kirk, has over the years turned into the adjectival phrase, "learning disabled children/adults", which somehow implies a global, pervasive condition, whereas in reality only certain learning processes are affected.

Now let's look at some practical definitions.

Defining Terms

Instead of starting with some very formal definitions of learning disabilities, I would rather relegate formal definitions to Appendix A, and keep this guide as informal as possible. I would prefer to present you with a more practical definition, in the form of characteristics that will make it obvious to you that a student has learning disabilities.

As I said earlier, I was fortunate to have Dr. Margie Golick working with me as a consultant on this book. She has kindly allowed me to quote the excellent definition of learning disabilities she used in her 1988 report to the Maritime Provinces Higher Education Commission, entitled *Learning Disabilities in Post-Secondary Education.* To avoid reinventing the wheel, I will quote it verbatim.

"For close to a hundred years, psychologists and physicians have described individuals who were puzzling and paradoxical in their learning ability, who could master complex ideas, but seemed intractable and hopeless in their inability to learn some 'simple' skills.

"Teachers were baffled by obviously bright children and adolescents who could not learn to read or spell. 'How can a kid who's so smart be so dumb?' said one teacher, indicating that nothing in her own teaching had prepared her for atypical learning patterns.

"To describe these puzzling students, the term 'learning disabilities' evolved. It was used to describe a number of different kinds of handicaps that can lead to discrepancies in a child's or adult's abilities. These may include any or all of the following:

1 Problems in processing information (visual, auditory, spoken or written verbal material);

2 Problems in memory (immediate memory; rote memory, memory for words, capacity for imagery, memory for sequences);

3 Difficulties in receptive and expressive language;

4 Problems in visual-motor integration;

5 Problems in spatial orientation;

6 Organizational problems—keeping track of details, keeping track of time.

"Students with learning disabilities, depending on the particular constellation of symptoms, or on local custom may be characterized as 'dyslexic', said to have 'perceptual motor problems', 'attention deficit disorder', or minimal brain dysfunction.

"Learning disabilities, which can affect even highly intelligent children, inevitably interfere with progress at school. They can cause difficulties in learning to read, write, spell and do mathematics. They can affect students in other less obvious ways. Students with learning disabilities may become frustrated, depressed, and bewildered at their learning problems, and might even have difficulty learning the social and recreational skills that would help to make life pleasurable outside of school.

"In the nearly three decades that the term has been widely used throughout the world, there has been controversy over the definition, over estimates of prevalence (with estimates ranging from 2% to 30% of the population), over the concept itself ('Is it a learning disability or a teaching disability?'). There has also been an enormous amount of research on the nature of the disabilities, on causes, on early identification, assessment techniques, on remedial methods, and on outcome of various treatment techniques.

"Both Canada and the United States have official definitions that are comprehensive but somewhat unwieldy. The following is a pragmatic account of learning disabilities:

1 The term is never used to characterize a 'slow learner' whose disabilities are more pervasive. Students with 'learning disabilities' have striking abilities and talents that contrast with the difficulties they have in some areas.

2 The problem is biological, reflecting some neurological dysfunction or a difference that affects the way information is processed, i.e. registered and remembered.

3 The disorder is permanent.

4 A large part of the treatment is educational. It consists of finding alternate ways to teach the skills that are hard to learn, of helping students with deficits in memory, language, reading, or writing to develop compensatory strategies, and of offering them accommodations that permit full participation in the classroom.

5 In many cases the processing problems persist and students, even after excellent remedial help, continue to have difficulties with reading, spelling, and written expression.

6 In spite of persistent problems, many students with learning disabilities continue their education at the post-secondary level, and go on to satisfying careers.

7 Many who have the potential for post-secondary education never get there because their learning disability has not been identified. They have been misjudged as unintelligent and guided into non-academic programs. Or they have dropped out of schools that were not meeting their needs.

[The same applies to adult students who have the potential for secondary education.]

8 Links have been made between learning disabilities and suicide and between learning disabilities and crime. The data are not clear, but certainly there are enormous frustrations for individuals whose abilities are untapped, who are harassed for difficulties they cannot help, who are accused of laziness or slothfulness when they are working enormously hard. What is clear is the importance of recognizing a potentially handicapping condition that can be helped, and the enormous waste of potential if it is not."

The origins of learning disabilities are in the brain. In normal cognitive function, the brain is continuously monitoring multiple sources of information, including internal body system functions and sensory information from the outside world. The brain sorts out all this information, ignoring much of it, but saving some of it in an organized fashion, in memory, for future use. The brain processes the information and decisions are made as to whether a response is required. If so, the brain organizes the response. For example, the eye blinks to avoid an approaching object, before a conscious decision is made to duck.

In people with learning disabilities there may be some kind of distortion of information in some parts of the brain. The distortion can cause deficits in perception, visual and auditory sequencing, spatial relations, memory, etc., and is frequently reflected in language, organizational and reasoning problems. Author Dale Brown, who often writes about her own learning disabilities, compared the distortion to fine tuning a radio, saying that at times information comes in loud and clear, but at other times, it is erratic and garbled.

Five to ten percent is a reasonable estimate of the population affected by learning disabilities, and the prevalence is clearly somewhat higher among socioeconomically disadvantaged populations, and higher in males than in females. More recently, however, the scales have been tipping, and we have been seeing almost equal numbers of men and women.

Most studies of the prevalence of learning disabilities have been of preadolescent populations. A few follow-up studies of affected children state that most continue to have related problems as adults. More research is necessary to confirm this hypothesis. However, the notion that a child will "grow out of it" is certainly no longer acceptable.

Whenever we teach adults with reasonable intelligence, who in spite of their intelligence, had enormous difficulties with conventionally presented information during their schooling, we can suspect that learning disabilities played a part. And because learning disabilities do not disappear with maturity, these adults are still encountering difficulties absorbing material presented in the conventional manner. Many have problems with reading, and surface as literacy students. Despite the sea of print that surrounds them, they are still not reading, writing, or spelling well enough to get by in their day-to-day lives. Often their lack of literacy skills has kept them from progressing in their jobs; they have been offered promotions because of their outstanding ability, but have not accepted because they fear the paperwork involved. One bright, articulate and bubbly student I know has been a seamstress at a department store for many years. On several occasions, she was offered a buyer's job. Each time she turned it down.

Other students are still encountering such basic problems with math that they are unable to count their change, tell time, budget or do their own banking. Their disabilities result in math problems, often referred to as dyscalculia.

According to the Learning Disabilities Association of Canada (LDAC), we cannot say that the majority of those who have learning disabilities are functionally illiterate, or that the majority of those who are functionally illiterate have learning disabilities. The exact statistical correlation has not been fully explored. However, there is no question that those who work in the literacy field should be aware of learning disabilities and their effect on learning to read. It is my impression that nearly half our students have learning disabilities, therefore it is imperative that we all understand the issues related to learning disabilities.

Clearly, there is a relationship between learning disabilities and illiteracy. In its position paper on illiteracy, the LDAC makes the following recommendations:

"...that post-secondary institutions actively combat illiteracy through the training of professionals and paraprofessionals in effective education services including remediation and accommodation for people with learning disabilities.

"...that all literacy programs provide comprehensive training for service providers to ensure effective educational services for people with learning disabilities."

For more specific information on how learning disabilities may manifest themselves in literacy or basic education students, I have included the following checklist. The adult with learning disabilities who has had normal educational opportunities will exhibit a constellation of these characteristics, but certainly not all of them.

Reading Skills

~ slow, laboured reading

~ poor comprehension

~ poor retention

~ difficulty identifying important points and/or main ideas

~ difficulty recalling sequence

~ poor mastery of phonics

[The most common complaints I get from students I suspect of having learning disabilities are, "I read, but I don't understand what I have read", or "I can't read (decode) the big words."]

Written Language Skills

~ poor penmanship

~ slow writing

~ difficulty with straight copying

~ difficulty with sentence structure

~ frequent spelling errors, including omissions, substitutions, transpositions

~ short compositions lacking development

Oral Language Skills

~ difficulty concentrating and comprehending

~ difficulty expressing what the student clearly knows, feels or understands

~ oral expression better than written (or vice versa)

~ difficulty with grammar

~ difficulty telling a story in proper sequence

~ difficulty listening and writing notes at the same time

~ tendency to misinterpret subtleties in language, tone of voice, or social situations

Mathematical Skills

~ incomplete mastery of basic facts

~ reversal of numbers

~ confusion of operational symbols

~ problems incorrectly copied

~ difficulty recalling the sequence of operational processes

~ difficulty understanding and retaining terms for mathematical concepts

~ difficulty comprehending word problems

~ reasoning deficits

~ associated disorders, such as problems with left-right orientation and directionality

Organizational and Study Skills

~ time management difficulties

~ slow to start and complete tasks

~ difficulty following oral and written directions

~ poorly organized written notes and compositions

~ short attention span

~ inefficient memorization and self-rehearsal strategies

~ often disoriented, late, or unusually early for appointments

Chapter 1

The Rich and the Famous

The Rich and the Famous

Many students with learning disabilities go on to post-secondary education and/or successful careers. In fact, some even become rich and famous. In the February 1986 issue of *Psychology Today*, an article titled "Facing the Invisible Handicap" cites the following examples:

"Many accomplished scholars, politicians, artists, entertainers, entrepreneurs, athletes and professionals have had to struggle with learning disabilities. Serious weaknesses in one area seem to spur some people on to develop exceptional strengths in other areas. The extra energy of hyperactive individuals, for example, can come in handy once it is put under control.

"Albert Einstein would probably be diagnosed as learning disabled if he were growing up today. He showed no signs of genius in his early years; his parents and teachers feared he was less than normal intellectually. It has been reported that he did not learn to talk until he was four years old nor read until he was nine, and he failed his entrance exam the first time he applied to the Federal Institute of Technology. In his own words, 'As a pupil I was neither particularly good nor bad. My principal weakness was a poor memory and especially a poor memory for words and texts.' One of his problems—and, ironically, his later claim to fame—was that he either could not or would not solve scientific and mathematical problems in the usual ways. Instead he invented his own unique, creative ways of conceptualizing problems.

"Today the young Thomas Edison probably would be recognized as dyslexic, but during his childhood he was simply thought of as stupid. 'I remember I used to never be able to get along at school. I was always at the foot of the class...my father thought I was stupid, and I almost decided that I was a dunce.' Eventually he was withdrawn from formal schools and tutored at home by his mother. He never did learn to spell or write grammatically; at the age of 19, he wrote to his mother: 'Started the Store several weeks. I have grown considerably I dont look much like a Boy now—Hows all the folk did you receive a Box of Books from Memphis that he promised to send them—languages. Your son Al.' [Edison's middle name was Alva.]

"Sculptor Auguste Rodin had difficulty learning to read and write. His father said, 'I have an idiot for a son,' and his uncle agreed, 'He is ineducable.'

"President Woodrow Wilson didn't learn his letters until he was nine years old or learn to read until he was 11.

"General George Patton never learned to read well and is said to have gotten through West Point by memorizing whole lectures.

"Other historical notables now thought to have been learning disabled include Vice-President Nelson Rockefeller, Leonardo da Vinci and Hans Christian Andersen."

Public figures who admit to having a learning disability include actresses Whoopi Goldberg and Cher, sportscaster and former Olympic decathlon winner Bruce Jenner and newscaster Peter Jennings. They have spoken publicly about their learning disabilities, urging others to feel more hopeful.

Actor Tom Cruise has talked candidly about his learning disabilities. "I was put in remedial reading classes. It was a drag. It separated you and singled you out." He compensated for his poor school performance by excelling first at all forms of sports and later by becoming an actor with exceptional self-discipline. "I enjoy the pressure of making a movie. It's like getting psyched up for a wrestling match—but with higher stakes. I thrive on it."

Child psychiatrist, Larry Silver, himself a dyslexic, is the former Acting Director of the National Institute of Mental Health, and is now a professor of psychiatry at Georgetown University and a renowned expert on learning disabilities. Dr. Silver wrote a book for parents of children with learning disabilities, The *Misunderstood Child*. He is quoted in *Psychology Today*:

"You should have seen the first draft of this book—spelling errors, letter reversals, illegible handwriting. But I have something now that I didn't have when I was in school. I have a secretary who has learned to read my handwriting, who can spell, and who no longer laughs at my errors ...

"My grades in elementary and junior high school were less than good...somehow I got my act together in high school. I taught myself how to learn and how to pass exams. That, for me, was the beginning. The ending never comes. I still face new frustrations and challenges. Recently I was at a Congressional hearing related to budget. I needed to pass information to someone who was answering a senator's questions. When I got my note back, on top it said 'Thanks'—then he proceeded to correct two spelling errors and one reversal."

Actress and singer Cher speaks out candidly about her school difficulties, and admits she still cannot make a long-distance call, because she cannot remember a string of 11 numbers. Nonetheless, she has managed to overcome, or compensate for, the obvious challenge of learning her lines.

Another entertainer who has learning disabilities, or learning difficulties as they call them in England, is British actress Susan Hampshire. Best known for her Emmy award-winning performances in "The Forsythe Saga", "The First Churchills" and "Vanity Fair", she has managed to portray her life as a dyslexic by writing (with the help of a secretary) a rather interesting account of her struggle with reading. It is published by St. Martin's Press in New York, and available in bookstores. *Susan's Story* makes easy and enjoyable reading for the tutor, and possibly some upper level literacy students as well. It might be an interesting idea to read parts of it to your student, if he cannot read it on his own. Her latest book is entitled *Every Letter Counts* (Bantam, 1990).

There are many less famous dyslexics who are successful. Many professionals and business people have worked around their problems with print, and have become successful in their jobs and careers.

Identifying Adults With Learning Disabilities

Identifying Adults With Learning Disabilities

Learning disabilities are prevalent throughout the general population. They touch the rich, the poor, everyone in between, and people of all races and religions. Learning disabilities affect native English speakers as well as immigrants. Those who are classed as culturally deprived and economically disadvantaged may suffer from learning disabilities as well. There is also a high percentage of people with learning disabilities among the prison population. As mentioned before—and this is an important point—while learning disabilities affect those of below-average, average and above-average intelligence, it is common to see learning disabilities manifested in potentially average, average and above average students.

One of the quickest ways of identifying an adult with learning disabilities is to assess the student's school history. If he seems to exhibit normal intelligence, has spent a number of years in school plagued by learning problems, and has now come to you because he cannot read, write or spell satisfactorily, you should suspect learning disabilities, and investigate.

People with learning disabilities are not a homogeneous group. Although their complaints may be similar—great difficulty in learning at school—they may have very different disabilities: different in kind, in number and in severity. Language difficulties, however, are fairly common, and therefore are another way of identifying adults with learning disabilities. Language may be less well-developed, with problems showing up in the areas of pronunciation, vocabulary or syntax.

In some cases, the language difficulty may be the result of problems in auditory processing. Spoken language goes by too quickly to be registered and remembered, so people with auditory processing disabilities miss much of what is said to them and are slower to notice nuances of the language and exceptions to rules. They are also slower to learn the details and intricacies of their language. In other cases, there may be some specific deficit in language learning ability. Any or all of the above difficulties may affect all language-related activities. Students with language problems typically have difficulties expressing themselves in speech and in writing, tend to miss some of what is said to them, and may misunderstand or miss the point of what they read.

Both speech difficulties and problems related to auditory perception should lead you to suspect learning disabilities. If a student has difficulty answering your questions or following what you say, it may indicate the existence of an auditory problem, which invariably leads to learning problems such as difficulties in spelling. If the student has trouble expressing his thoughts, it may indicate an organizational problem that will manifest itself not only in speech but elsewhere as well, causing learning difficulties. Some students will speak inappropriately or be inattentive, while others will have difficulty following verbal instructions. All these difficulties, of course, make learning a problem.

Memorization problems, which are also prevalent in students with learning disabilities, show up in a variety of ways: for example, an inability to memorize the alphabet, learn number facts by heart, or recognize sight words. Socially, the student may not be able to remember the names of people he meets or recall common facts in conversation. Memory can be affected in a number of ways. These include immediate memory, long-term memory, recall of rote arbitrary material as opposed to meaningful material, memory for facts, the ability to revisualize words, as well as the capacity for new learning. There may also be problems with the retrieval of material that has been learned. Any memory difficulty may be specific to one modality, and may be different for verbal material or for visual or even kinaesthetic learning. Inevitably, a student's inefficient memory compromises his ability to learn and to function normally in a world that is full of important information that must be stored in the brain.

Another signal of learning disabilities is a significant discrepancy between a student's verbal and written performance. "But he *sounds* so bright," is the often-heard refrain about a student suspected of having learning disabilities. And he often is, but he is unable to deal effectively with print, the most common medium of education in our society. In my work with literacy students, I am finding a growing number of these students coming forward for help in reading and writing. Their verbal skills and intelligence have often helped them get through high school, but they get stuck when the demands of a job or junior college or university require a high level of reading and writing. Increasing literacy publicity brings them to our door, literally begging for help.

When reading, students often complain of visual problems. They may complain of severe eye fatigue. Or they may complain that the words never seem to look the same from day to day: on a bad day, a student seems unable to read words he could read just the day before. The words may appear to jump around on a page, making it virtually impossible to read. Students also speak of words being scrambled and letters being reversed. Understandably, they often misread and miscopy words.

Another sign is uneven performance in general; the student seems to do well in some areas, but has a great difficulty in one specific area. I have seen many literacy students who are capable of doing high school or college math, and perhaps science, and are in fact taking classes at either one of those levels, but are still having trouble with basic reading and writing.

A similar example is the adult who is good at visual-spatial skills, such as drawing and design, but is unable to memorize spelling patterns. I once had such a student. Elaine was reasonably intelligent, could read fairly well, and was an outstanding artist. But her spelling and writing skills were extremely poor. She wanted desperately to go on to high school, and finally gave it a try. Unfortunately, her writing and spelling skills pulled her down, discouraging her until she finally gave up. Getting a "good" job was almost impossible for Elaine, who really needed that high school diploma. When I last saw her, she was doing odd jobs like babysitting, hoping that things would improve.

Spelling seems to be an area of great difficulty and never-ending frustration. While reading improves with instruction, spelling often continues to plague students with learning disabilities. Fortunately, there are several ways that bad spellers can compensate for spelling, which I will talk about later.

Getting ideas down on paper is no easy task even for the best of writers. For the students we are concerned with, writing is extremely difficult. For one thing, organizational problems may hamper them; for another, they are sure to be intimidated by their poor spelling and handwriting abilities. Sentence structure, punctuation and self-correcting tend to be problems as well. In general, written work will often fail to express students' ideas, or their understanding. Because writing usually lags a level or two behind reading, and sometimes even more, it is not surprising to find reluctant writers among adults with learning disabilities.

Hyperactivity, hypoactivity, and attention deficits are common symptoms in adults with learning disabilities. Sometimes hyperactivity serves them well in life, permitting them to be extremely hardworking and productive. Hypoactivity and attentional deficits certainly don't help them; in fact, they most certainly curtail effective learning and productivity.

Left-right confusions, organizational problems and generalization difficulties are also common problems faced by these adults. Actress Susan Hampshire often refers to these problems in her book, stating how on many occasions they managed to foul up her day-to-day life and her career. The minor task of arriving at a new place on time for an audition was a major trauma for this multi-talented performer, who could memorize lines but could not follow simple directions.

Once again, it is important to note that no student will manifest all or even most of the signs of learning disabilities. Of course, any of the above signs in a student may not necessarily mean he has learning disabilities. Observe the student over the course of time and look for a clustering or pattern of several of these deficits, then investigate.

Studies have shown that a significant number of people with dyslexia have a family history of reading or language disorders, indicating a hereditary (genetic) component. There are documented accounts of Scottish clans whose members experience delayed speech and reading and writing difficulties. Those of us who work with adults with learning disabilities often hear that their children are experiencing similar difficulties in school.

Now let's look at some profiles of adults with learning difficulties:

Bob experiences severe memory problems. He has had difficulty learning things most adults (and children) learn with ease: the days of the week, the months of the year, and times tables. A major problem is his inability to master spelling. These problems have caused Bob considerable difficulties in school and on the job. Bob says humorously, "I'm a slow learner and a fast forgetter."

Ellen has visual spatial motor co-ordination problems. She has been labelled a "klutz". She has difficulty putting keys in locks, opening milk cartons and hitting a ball. All sports cause problems for Ellen. These difficulties have led to Ellen feeling less secure about herself than she should.

In the group of people like Ellen, there is a disproportionate number of left-handed or ambidextrous people. In fact, this holds true for people with learning disabilities in general.

The following examples are taken from the same *Psychology Today* article we looked at above.

"Jane has different problems, created by a poor sense of spatial orientation. She is always getting lost, has no sense of direction and cannot tell right from left. Simple acts such as tying her own shoes or finding a numbered room in an office building present serious challenges. Part of the problem involves knowing where her body is in the surrounding space. This ability comes to most of us automatically without thought. But Jane is forever bumping into walls and people, dropping things or tripping on steps unless she watches her every movement.

"Many people with learning disabilities don't even realize they have them. They and others attribute their actions or deficiencies to some other cause. One young man always gets lost on trips, can never find his car in the parking lot and constantly drops things. He has come to think of himself as clumsy or careless, both misleading labels which imply that he just isn't trying very hard to organize himself and his body movements. The truth may be that his brain does not analyze spatial relations well.

"An artistic young woman I know can only communicate well verbally with great effort. Most people simply assume that she is shy when in fact, her reluctance to talk comes from built-in 'static' in her verbal communication channel. To compensate, she has developed her capacity to express her feelings in visual images. While she feels comfortable with this solution, it often leaves her hungry for closeness with other people.

"Some people's learning disabilities show up in ways that are easy to confuse with various types of psychopathology. A young woman may be considered depressed because of her sparse speech and slow movements; in fact, she has an inherited motor coordination problem that requires her to speak and move slowly to maintain good control over her muscles.

"A friendly, eager young man seems unable to control his impulsiveness and constantly makes social blunders. His therapist has concluded that his social problems originate in some inner conflicts about relationships with others that make him anxious or aggressive in social situations. The truth may be that his problems stem from the biologically based hyperactivity he has experienced in one form or another since infancy."

Chapter 3

How Learning Disabilities Affect Adults

How Learning Disabilities Affect Adults

In 1988, I found the following story in the LDAC publication, *National*:

The Ropes That Bind, *by Bastion dePeuter*

"Soon after my eleventh birthday I was allowed to accompany my uncle into town to attend the opening of a new feed-mill. On arrival we saw a huge elephant in the parking lot. I noticed that he was tied with only a half inch nylon rope by his right front foot to a skinny little fence post.

"Later, I overheard one of the farmers ask the man who was with the elephant, 'Do you expect that little post and rope to hold him if he were to get a notion to leave?' 'No,' said the man with the elephant, 'If I were to put a harness on him, he might be able to pull down that whole building. But you see, when he was captured in India as a baby, the people who trained him put a metal shackle and chain on his leg. The baby elephant tried again and again to break free but couldn't. After a while, he just accepted the idea that he couldn't get free. As long as he feels something on his leg, he won't move. It is purely psychological.'

"I am a lot like that elephant. I'd failed at learning so often that I believed I couldn't learn. I have only recently gone back to pull on the rope."

This story by an adult with learning disabilities illustrates what some of these adults go through. Ashamed, embarrassed and broken, they label themselves as stupid and resist remediation for a long time. Many are just beginning to return to school to improve their education. Instructing these adults is a relatively new concept.

Only recently have psychologists and educators realized that learning disabilities are not a problem that children outgrow. The adult may mask the handicap, but still remains impaired. Learning disabilities have almost as great an impact on social and emotional development as on education. Because the symptoms are so easy to misdiagnose, many adults grow up misunderstanding their problems, thereby failing to get the remediation and *support* they need. They state that they thought of themselves as dumb or retarded until they were diagnosed as being dyslexic. All these conditions lead to varying degrees of emotional scarring, which later require some kind of psychological intervention.

A tutor's support and the support of the student's family are invaluable. Remind your students that learning disabilities are only one slice of their identity, and encourage them to focus on the more successful and positive aspects of their lives. If, however, serious problems persist in the area of self-esteem and confidence, do not hesitate to speak to your student about getting professional help.

While most professionals agree that social adjustment problems are common in adults with learning disabilities, this area has not received sufficient attention. And while the focus on learning disabilities has traditionally been in the area of education, the consequences are rarely confined to school or even work. Many areas in life are affected, such as relationships with family and friends, confidence and self-image and non-academic pastimes such as cultural activities and sports.

It is also said that in 20% of cases, learning disabilities do not occur in the areas of language, abstraction, math or problem-solving, but rather in psycho-social areas. In their social lives, these students may observe less, misperceive more, and not learn easily from their life experiences. They tend to have difficulties reading social cues and facial expressions. They may also act inappropriately because they don't know the verbal routines that make for easy social interaction.

Diagnosis

Diagnosis

Testing and evaluation should be left to professionals. These may include psychologists, psychometricians or trained educators. With the help of standardized tests that measure aptitude and achievement, as well as tests which evaluate information processing, qualified professionals can judge whether a student has learning disabilities. In the case of adults, they also take into consideration such things as school history and work performance.

A psychoeducational evaluation is a complex process, and the assessment of adults differs from the assessment of children. No single battery of tests exists which identifies adults with learning disabilities, nor is there consensus on which tests should be used.

There is, however, agreement about the fact that informal measures are helpful. For instance, at higher educational levels, notes and term papers are evaluated. Dr. Loring Brinckerhoff, an expert in the field, humorously cited an informal test he developed to assess hyperactivity. He seated his students in a swivel chair and then counted the number of rotations they made during the course of their evaluation.

Each case may differ because of the student's current concerns, questions and goals, and testing has to address each student's particular issues.

As the tutor comes to terms with the fact that the field of learning disabilities is not an exact science, and like the disability itself, is somewhat fuzzy, she will feel more comfortable with the idea of addressing the specific problems with remediation, rather than concentrating on establishing a definitive diagnosis.

Chapter 5

Identifying Specific Problems and Determining Educational Needs

Identifying Specific Problems and Determining Educational Needs

Finding the student's problems and making provision for remediation are tied together in this chapter because they are intricately related, and because seeing the two together will help the tutor plan remediation. I particularly liked what Dr. Loring Brinckerhoff said recently at a learning disabilities lecture that I attended. Poor academic achievement by these students was not due to mental retardation, lack of opportunity, emotional disturbance, lack of motivation, or visual or auditory acuity, but rather 'disteachia'. In other words, good teaching can make the difference!

We will deal with further aspects of remediation in the following chapter. But remember that these two chapters are not intended as a cookbook of educational solutions—only helpful suggestions of things that often work. You will have to use not only all that you have learned so far about education and your student, but also your best judgement—and perhaps a dash of instinct.

The identification of specific problems can be much more difficult in adults than it is in children. For one thing, adults may mask their disabilities or compensate. For another, the area of adult learning disabilities is relatively new, and few educational diagnostic tools are available. Experienced educators and psychologists must use or adapt assessment tools developed for children, or use their own interpretative skills to tease out information from adults. Fortunately, many adults are good self-reporters, so in-depth interviews are extremely useful. Patterns of strengths and weaknesses can be gleaned from all these sources, and remediation can be planned. Psychological assessments can be very helpful but are not essential to determine educational problems and plan remediation.

An interview format and questionnaire developed by Dr. Margie Golick for use with adults is included in Appendix D. It is an excellent tool for the literacy coordinator or tutor. It will take several hours to complete, but you should be able to make a rough approximation of the student's intelligence, identify a number of learning difficulties particular to that student, and assess his strengths and motivation. The student's abilities and disabilities can be teased out with remediation in mind, and compensatory strategies and accommodations can be planned.

The literacy practitioner should feel comfortable with the assessment questionnaire, since it is similar to those designed to individualize instruction; however, if questions arise, it would be advisable to get in touch with a learning disabilities professional.

For the student who has questioned his ability in the past and is now anxious and frustrated about his inability to learn, an in-depth diagnosis can give both tutor and student an understanding of why he has not achieved in the past and alert him to the specific nature of his disability. This will not only be a relief ("I'm not stupid after all!") but will also help the student take a more organized approach to learning. Once he knows his strengths and weaknesses, he will have a concrete basis on which to build.

Language

Specific characteristics such as the following not only identify students with learning disabilities, but also clearly indicate areas that need remediation: language problems that include mispronunciation, grammatical errors, and limited vocabulary. An interview with a student will likely elicit other specific language problems, such as difficulty understanding complex sentences.

Recognizing the problems, discussing them with your student and deciding together which ones should be worked on will give you a basis for many lessons. Student input is as important here as anywhere else. Students may need help in building their vocabulary and in using a variety of sentence structures. If your student is language deficient, he should be taught a number of language skills in an orderly and systematic way. Sources of information for the tutor and exercises for the student may be found in English second-language teaching materials, such as the *Laubach Way to English* books.

Auditory processing problems, including difficulty understanding instructions, difficulty discriminating sounds (e.g. consonant clusters at the beginning of words) and difficulty with auditory retrieval (e.g. remembering names) can also be identified in an interview. Suggestions for remediation would include speaking slowly so as not to overload the student, speaking in small chunks where possible, and repeating important information as often as possible—without sounding too repetitive. This may take a little creativity.

Another useful technique is to explore the vocabulary your student encounters verbally and in text. Find the words and terms he does not know, tailoring lessons to his needs. What surer route could there be to educational success than tailoring lessons to students' needs?

Vocabulary tests can measure the richness of a student's vocabulary. If you are unable to obtain a test, listen to the student's language and judge for yourself. Does the student know the names of things, common words for everyday items? Is his language varied? Does he have words to express shades of meaning? For instance, can he distinguish between walk, shuffle, amble, and saunter? Does he know not only animal names, but names of their young (e.g. calf, kitten, puppy)? Does he know names of parts of things—not just ladder but rung, not just table but leg? Does he use accurate words for qualities of experience—tough, slippery, slimy, etc.? Does he use abstract terms—words for feelings? A good educator will be able to judge what the student knows and where he needs enrichment.

The student's expressive language, which is indicative of his language abilities in general, is intricately related to his reading ability. The thing that stands out most in my mind after working with literacy students for the past 16 years is that those who have language deficits are generally poorer readers than those who have better language skills. Unfortunately, poor language skills engender further language problems. Activities designed to enrich language such as games, discussions, and vocabulary exercises, can be planned according to the student's needs. Upper level students can be taught how to use a thesaurus, dictionary and grammar checker to improve their writing.

Writing

Another simple diagnostic technique is to evaluate the student's handwriting. Typically, it will look childish and may contain any combination of the following problems: 'b' substituted for 'd' or vice versa; a mix of cursive writing and print; poorly formed letters; writing sprawled unevenly across the page; spelling errors, particularly little words like *the, who, of, from,* etc.; incorrect homonyms; an inappropriate mix of capital and small letters; or omissions. It may look immature due to many cross-outs, write-overs and erasures. The following example is typical of student writing.

Sample of Writing

I have read your artlic in a mozine, I have learning disable I only found out 3 year ago my reading level was at a 2 to3 Level. I have been trying to teach my self.

I'm trying too going back to school at : colege collage, and told abrut my learning disable, they said they can not help me all all I was the fisst person with a learning disable, So they told me to a trouter but I have not heard from him again.

All the above problems and other similar ones can be remediated as they arise in student writing. Since the student should be writing as often as possible, at least once every lesson, errors will come up. As they do, point them out to your student and plan a lesson around them if necessary. Be careful not to overwhelm the student: work with small chunks of information at a time. Ideally, teach one or at the most two skills in a writing lesson, and reinforce these new concepts at various intervals.

Common mechanical errors students make include misplaced commas and periods, inappropriate capital and small letters, sentence fragments, run-on sentences, misplaced modifiers, faulty pronoun references, and incorrect homonyms (my favourite is "toed" for "towed"). Each of these kinds of errors can then become lesson topics. Work on the weak areas, but be sure to point out areas of strength to your student and compliment him on his progress. Praise will encourage your student to work harder, and give him the type of support and confidence he has probably experienced seldomly.

Help your student choose appropriate but simple writing lessons such as narratives, which are simplest to handle because they can be structured in chronological order. Progress to more difficult lessons later, when the student's confidence and writing have improved.

Help the student to organize the material, teaching such techniques as a jot outline, topic sentences, logical transitions, etc. Above all, encourage him to read his material to see whether it makes sense and reads well. Encourage him to strike out unnecessary words and repetitious phrases.

When writing, many students with learning disabilities often confine themselves to simple words, yet convey their ideas reasonably well, evidencing good intelligence. They should be taught how to use various tools to enhance their vocabulary—for example, a thesaurus, dictionary, computer with spell checker, or hand-held spelling checker. See Appendix E for further information on computers, computer programs and the Franklin hand-held spelling checker.

A major problem for these students is their inability to proofread and self-correct. Stress to your student that the most important thing is to get his ideas down on paper, and make sure they are conveying what he wants to convey. When it all makes sense, give him a chance to proofread and self-correct, looking up words he is not sure of, substituting more appropriate words when necessary, rearranging sentences and inserting the proper punctuation. Give him as many tools to work with as possible. A computer with a good word-processing program is a valuable tool for these students.

Remind him that you won't always be around to help, and encourage him to follow hunches. Explain that every good writer uses a thesaurus and a dictionary. Allow him to edit and rewrite his work several times until he is satisfied with it: the essence of writing is rewriting.

When the student has self-corrected all he can on his own, it is time for you to help him find the errors he could not find. An interesting technique is to mark each line that has an error and ask the student to find and correct the errors. Later, when the student has become skilled at finding errors in the marked lines, mark only paragraphs with errors and have him track them down. At first, you can add clues such as the type of mistake or the number of mistakes; later on, omit the clues. This type of practice may help a student improve his editing skills. Other editing techniques include re-reading the text slowly, pointing to every word, reading the text onto a tape and listening to it for things that do not make sense, and reading the text backwards to check for spelling errors. When we read forwards, our brain fills in what our hand has left out, especially if we are very familiar with the material. When all this is done, have your student do what most of us do—ask another adult to proofread the material.

Help your student with unfamiliar concepts or rules, or problems he is unable to solve. This is a good time for remediation.

Spelling

Spelling errors vary. They may be gross errors, demonstrating little resemblance between the sight and sound of words, or smaller errors in common everyday words. Reversals, repetition of letters and omitted endings are common.

To find your student's weaknesses, give him several spelling dictations—more than likely, he's avoiding problem words when writing. Are his errors related to reversals? Does he rely on logical phonetic alternatives, e.g. "hart" instead of "heart"? Are his errors the result of not knowing the spelling rules? Are his problems related to poor auditory processing? In other words, are sounds scrambled or missing? Are parts of words added to words? An example: "disabilitities" for "disabilities", which I have typed (and corrected) numerous times in this text (the result, in my case, of terrible typing skills).

After you have determined your student's weak areas, plan appropriate remediation. If he needs spelling rules, teach them as sequentially as you can, stressing their importance. It is possible that your student was not given enough rules in school. There was a time during the '60s when content was the only thing that mattered, and rules and the three Rs went out the window.

The kinaesthetic approach works well when trying to remediate stubborn spelling problems. An effective way to learn new spelling words is to write each word three times, simultaneously spelling each of them out loud while writing. Both the writing and the spelling aloud are crucial to the learning process.

Encourage students to look carefully at words, to be sure that they have all the parts of the word down, they have missed none of the letters they thought should be there, and they have put all the letters down in the right order. Paying attention to the meaning of the word is also a helpful strategy—for example, the word "signature" has "sign" in it. Paying attention to how words look visually is another technique, such as words within words (fat/her).

Practice still makes perfect in spelling, so practice, despite the fact that it is boring at times, should be stressed in the form of continual review and "work" on errors. Of course, it helps to make practice fun. Therefore any games you can incorporate into the lesson (for example, Scrabble) will make the learning more palatable.

Phonics

Most literacy programs have good diagnostic procedures (e.g. word analysis tests) that help identify which phonic skills the student has mastered and which he has not. This type of evaluation should be used to track missing skills that can then be taught in logical order, thereby satisfying the student's need for structure and organization. The student who does not have good phonic skills will undoubtedly need them as he progresses; he will need good decoding skills to unlock the multisyllable words that are frequently seen at higher reading levels. One of the most common complaints I get from upper level students is, "I can't read the big words." All the knowledge and experience they bring to the page don't seem to be enough; neither are predictive skills or syntactical cues. They don't need a whole language approach, they need help with the one skill they have yet to master—phonics.

Phonics programs are highly recommended for adults with learning disabilities because they have been a strong component of most successful programs for dyslexic children. Laubauch's approach is phonics-oriented, providing that components such as *Focus on Phonics* are used to supplement the skillbooks. When more remediation is needed, look to other sources to complement the Laubach books. Dr. Sybil Schwartz, formerly of the Montreal Children's Hospital, and professionals at the Learning Associates of Montreal recommend a program called *Words in Colour* because of its fresh approach: for the adult student, it is usually a brand-new approach, unlikely to be associated with past school failures. It is intellectually challenging and systematic, proceeding in small steps as it teaches reading and spelling simultaneously. And it helps students understand that the left-to-right arrangement of letters represents a series of sounds in time.

The phonics approach should, of course, be complemented with the reading of meaningful and interesting text.

Reading

Ask your student to read and analyze the cueing systems he is using. Is he using the syntactic cue system? Does he anticipate the word because he knows the expected order for words in a sentence? Does he use the semantic cue system? Does he anticipate the words because he knows their meaning and therefore knows what should and should not make sense? Does he decode well? Which of these systems work well for the student? Which need more work?

Test for comprehension, memory and sequencing ability by asking your student to retell the passage and answer questions about the story. Take note of the student's reading style. Does he read fluently or haltingly? Does he observe punctuation? Does he self-correct? Does he make good guesses? Which of these skills must be improved upon? Take detailed notes and discuss all these points with your student. Again, be sure to point out his strengths, reinforcing those abilities which will be helpful to him. You can't use the skill well unless you know you've got it. When I was first learning to swim as a child, a camp swim instructor told me that I was an excellent swimmer. I really wasn't quite excellent—at least not then—but being made aware that I was a good swimmer and enjoying that praise encouraged me to become a very good swimmer.

Memory

A digit span test such as the one in Appendix F, which is typical of digit span tests included in most intelligence tests, is helpful in detecting certain kinds of auditory processing problems. It can tell you how much information your student can take in at one time, and can also alert you to specific difficulties in appreciating sequential order. Very simply, it is a test in which several series of digits are read to the student who is asked to repeat them. The average adult can remember six digits. Any marked discrepancies suggest auditory processing problems. The digit span test can test attention, rote recall and immediate memory.

If auditory processing is a problem, the tutor is advised to speak in shorter chunks, repeat what he has to say and/or write instructions down. If the student is made aware of the problem, he can compensate by writing things down that he may not be able to store in his memory. Discussion between the tutor and student should generate a list of occasions when the student should automatically jot verbal communication down, for example telephone numbers, addresses, directions, and specific instructions at work. Your student might as well learn this skill. It's a skill we all need anyway after the age of 40, or is it 35?

Repetition

There are various other techniques that not only test the student's abilities, but also indicate appropriate teaching strategies for the tutor to use with the student. One formal test measures the ability to learn by repetition. However, the tutor need not know how to administer this test because you are apt to be seeing the student over a long period of time, so you can observe whether or not he learns by repetition and the number of repetitions it might take him to learn specific skills. If he recalls more and more with each repetition, he is obviously benefitting by the repetition. Repetition would then become a key teaching strategy. The challenge here is for the tutor to make the repetitive practice as interesting as possible.

Visual-Spatial Problems

Drawing tests can indicate visual-spatial problems. There are a number of tests on the market, easily administered and scored, that call for copying geometric forms. An informal task is to ask the student to draw a clock face with the hands set at a particular time, say twenty to seven. Does the clock look like a clock? Are the numbers equally spaced in their correct positions? Are the hands proportioned correctly, and pointing to the right numbers?

Psychologists often ask students to draw a human figure, and use a scoring system that indicates an adequate product. Tutors can informally gauge their student's drawing by noting the proportions, details, quality of line and general maturity. Drawings should look like a rough approximation of what they are supposed to be. If they look like modern art, something is wrong. Remediation is not recommended for this problem, but it is important for the tutor to be aware of it, because it might show up in the learning process. Rather than misdiagnosing it as laziness or another problem, recognize that this may be a true disability in your student.

Chapter 6

More About Remediation

More About Remediation

Teaching Techniques

Whole Language

Recommended teaching techniques include a variety of approaches. While the whole language approach is now highly recommended for children because of the richness of language it brings them, it has not always proven successful with dyslexic children. Normally, children who use the whole language approach begin to generalize how the language works. Many children with learning disabilities, however, do not. They must be taken aside and taught through an intellectual approach and through sound-symbol relationships. Because so little research has been done with adults, we can only *assume* they will follow suit, especially since many have been surrounded yet not helped by a language and print-rich environment. Interestingly enough, in the myriad of students I have met, the upper-level readers I suspect of having learning disabilities bear this theory out. They come to the initial interview asking if they can start at the beginning and proceed through all the levels to make sure there are no holes in their knowledge. They want to learn all the skills. Of course, you wouldn't give a level six reader beginning instruction, but you would perform diagnostic tests to find out just where those holes are.

While language experience has been shown to produce great writers, it does not always produce great readers. Too often, teachers are told not to concentrate on phonics in this approach, or assume that they should not. More school systems are now recognizing the gaps that phonics-deficient programs produced and are reinstating programs that teach the sounds of letters and letter groups.

Silent/Oral Reading

Listening to oral reading is a good way for the tutor to detect reading problems and to get the student to read every word. Silent reading, however, is generally more appropriate than oral reading. After all, why do adults need to read? If it's for information, silent reading is the skill they need. When reading silently, the student does not need to read every word to get the overall meaning. Point this out to your student.

It's not much use to practice the skill of oral reading, except perhaps for those who want to use it when reading bedtime stories to children. Students often want to practice oral reading because they remember it as something important they had to do in school.

Word Games and Tongue Twisters

While practice is recommended to gain fluency, practice is often boring. Adults, like children, must be encouraged to practice. Word games and tongue twisters seem to work with children. They enjoy the challenge. The same is true of adults. I recommend Dr. Golick's books, *Playing with Words* and *Whacky Word Games* available from Pembrooke Publishers, for this purpose. Although developed mainly for children with learning problems, it is full of games and ideas that are useful for adults. See Appendix G for the address of Pembrooke Publishers. Increased vocabulary and improved thinking skills are obvious spinoffs of games, tongue twisters, riddles, and such.

Low-Level, High-Interest Novels

I try to get adults to read as many low-level, high-interest novels as possible because they provide repetition of vocabulary. Unfortunately, at the lower levels, there aren't enough novels available. Publishers are just beginning to pay attention to this area, and reading councils across the country are just starting to produce their own novels.

Math

Math students must be taught to disentangle the math "language" before they can learn effectively. Terms such as "1/2 price" or "50% discount" may have little meaning to the learner and little relation to each other in his mind. Even simple terms such as "take away from" or "subtract" boggle some minds. These terms must be taught before teaching can be effective.

Phonics and Cue Systems

The underlying problem for many people with reading disorders— even words that have been studied repeatedly—is difficulty recognizing words. Therefore they will rely heavily on sounding out words. Naturally attention will be focused on decoding, resulting in poor comprehension.

Again, why do we read if not for comprehension? I mention this here because so many students come to us not realizing that fact, obvious as it may seem. Many come wanting to improve their oral reading, believing that is what reading is about.

Try to reinforce the idea of reading for meaning with your student. Concentrate on phonics instruction (decoding) with the student who needs more help than the whole language approach, with its mainstays of semantic and syntax cues. Your student will derive more meaning from the text when all three systems work well together.

Helpful Hints

Here's a list of ideas and techniques that many teachers find useful with students who have visual problems. Use those that seem appropriate to the adult's needs and prove to be successful:

~ Encourage your student to see an eye doctor (opthamologist) for an eye examination. Rule out any pathology in the eyes before assuming problems in the brain. If he wears glasses, have him ask the doctor if his prescription is still correcting his vision.

~ Use a solid-coloured, plain bookmark with the upper edge highlighted. It's useful for following while reading.

~ Supplement visual learning with auditory and tactile stimuli. There is evidence, for instance, that spelling is improved by incorporating auditory and tactile stimuli into spelling lessons.

~ Read directions aloud while pointing to them.

~ Have students repeat orally what they write.

~ Take advantage of the student's stronger modality by balancing the lesson with auditory instruction, e.g. listening, discussion and tapes.

~ Practise verbal recall of things your student has seen visually.

A student with auditory processing problems will have difficulty decoding unfamiliar multisyllable words. He may rely heavily on context clues and guessing to get the meaning. Again, a structured phonics program such as those in the *Laubach Skillbooks* or *Challenger* series will be useful. You may want to supplement these books with other phonics material.

Here's another list, this time of ideas and techniques to help people with auditory processing problems:

~ Encourage the student to visit an ear, nose and throat doctor (otolaryngologist) to arrange for a hearing test to make sure he does not have a hearing problem. Hearing problems are quite different from auditory processing problems such as poor auditory sequencing, memory and discrimination.

~ Work in a room without any auditory distractions.

~ Read passages of interest out loud to your student and practise listening comprehension.

~ Speak clearly and face your student during the lesson.

~ Use visual approaches that might help your student, e.g. sight words, language experience stories, and context clues.

~ Use taped materials such as books, programs you have taped, or tapes you have made as lessons.

~ Practice giving your student instructions, both orally and in written form.

- ~ Use word recognition techniques and structural analysis.
- ~ Stress configuration.
- ~ Use a microphone which the student tunes into through a headset, thus obscuring auditory distractions.

The Kinaesthetic Approach

The kinaesthetic approach is highly recommended for adults with learning disabilities. The more senses involved, the better the learning. Involve the auditory sense too (e.g. ask students to say and spell words out loud while tracing them). Writing and typing also help in learning. Stress the fact that the more senses involved, the better the learning. This may be a new concept for your student. Being aware of it can help him learn things when he is practising on his own.

Writing

The more a student writes, the better. Find ways to make writing an interesting and useful activity. Writing should be made less threatening and more tolerable. The adult student is especially likely to see the benefits of writing (e.g. letters to family, notes to teachers, letters of complaint, etc.). The section on technology presents a fresh approach to writing for those adults who have not yet investigated the computer.

Chapter 7

Attention and Concentration

Attention and Concentration

By now you have probably heard a great deal about attention deficit disorder (ADD) or attention deficit disorder with a hyperactive component (ADHD), as well as one of the drugs used to control these disorders, Ritalin.

Four to eight percent (4-8%) of school aged children suffer from ADD, which is actually more of a syndrome than a disorder. It is characterized by an inconsistent attention span. These children have trouble focusing or sustaining their attention on academic tasks, and ultimately miss chunks of their basic education.

More severe cases are controlled by Ritalin, which calms the child and allows her to have a more constant focus. Ritalin is helpful for 75-90% of the children who take it. While some adults fear taking Ritalin, others claim it brings things into focus like a pair of glasses.

While some children outgrow their attention difficulties, in others the difficulties remain. In fact, up to 3% of adults may have the disorder. Renowned individuals who are suspected of having ADD include Wolfgang Amadeus Mozart, Albert Einstein, George Bernard Shaw, and General Patton. Surprisingly, some adults with ADD are actually able to concentrate intensely (hyper-focus) when a subject captures their attention—but more often than not, they have difficulty in attending to a task or concentrating to a very high degree.

Adults who suffer from ADD may find it difficult to learn, especially in situations where there are multiple stimuli or tasks which overload the individual very quickly. However, the upside of ADD (and there *is* an upside) is that people with ADD have high energy, creativity, intuitiveness and enthusiasm. There are now several ADD Internet sites. They are full of first-hand accounts of living with the syndrome. See Appendix G for the addresses. You may wish to access them if you believe your student has ADD.

Dr. Lillian Hechtman is a professor of paediatrics and psychiatry at McGill University and the director of research at the Montreal Children's Hospital division of adolescent psychiatry. In her book, *Mapping the Maze*, Dr. Hechtman concludes there is still no reliable test for diagnosing ADD or ADHD. She recommends patient history as the primary diagnostic tool (see the chapter on diagnosis for Dr. Loring Brinckerhoff's informal yet innovative measure of hyperactivity). Diagnosis should, however, always be undertaken by a professional in the field. Call the psychiatric department of your local hospital, or consult a branch of the Learning Disabilities Association of Canada. They can provide you with the names of individuals who work in the field and who are qualified to diagnose adults.

Once it has been confirmed that your student suffers from ADD, be sure that she reads or hears about other people who have the disorder. Realizing that she is not alone will help her morale.

ADD itself does not lead to decoding problems, but many adults report that they find that they can't sustain attention to reading for long periods, and that they lose their concentration, which in turn affects comprehension.

Encouraging reading for meaning, and incorporating directed comprehension exercises, will help students with attention deficit disorders concentrate on comprehension. Ensuring that the student is fully engaged in reading in a distraction-free environment is paramount.

Use interesting materials and those which direct the student to look for specific details, such as the main idea, the sequence, the conclusion, etc. Or create materials appropriate to your student's needs and plan questions which encourage her to seek information that is meaningful to her.

Teach the student some strategies for attending to her reading material. This may include reading the text several times and for several reasons: to get a general sense; to get the main idea; to seek out specific details; to determine sequence, etc. It is important to note that these strategies may suit one student's needs, but a different set of strategies will better suit another. Help your student develop the strategies that are appropriate for her.

When teaching reading, change your lessons frequently to sustain your student's interest. Long periods of concentration on one lesson are difficult to sustain.

Assist the ADD student to increase her reading time. Teach her to sustain interest in text for increasingly longer periods of time by practising this skill. Be sure that she reaches an optimal length of time by aiming for small increments which ensure success.

Similar techniques apply to the area of writing. Handwriting can be improved once the student decides what suits her best—printing or cursive writing—and what kind of implement she is most comfortable using. Some students prefer typing or using a computer.

Once the mechanical part of writing is solved, students can pay more attention to the actual task of composition. In the beginning, assign small chunks of writing. Then teach your student to write longer compositions by adding more and relevant information to the smaller compositions. This way she will also be increasing her time-on-task. Recording the time-on-task, while successfully increasing the time, is one way for the student to measure her progress. Try this technique in other areas as well.

Some students will require more time to complete exercises, assignments and tests. By allowing the student to take the time she requires, she will be less anxious and more capable of attending to the actual writing. If the work is ultimately accomplished, how long it takes to do it should not be a limiting factor. This necessary accommodation is now widely used in universities.

Teach your student to seek out and work in distraction-free environments when writing. Writing requires a great deal of concentration, so any type of background noise (e.g. the television blaring, children playing, friends conversing) will limit the student's ability to concentrate.

Above all, take the time to explain the above strategies and accommodations to your student. Some students may look upon them as cheating—assure them that they are not. Explain—repeatedly if necessary—that everyone learns in different ways, and that different techniques help different people.

EWME

MEWEM

WMEMWEM

Irlen Syndrome

Some students with reading difficulties report that their problem is increased because of discomfort and fatigue which comes from looking at print. They find the page blurs, letters move, the white spaces appear too bright, and all of this distracts them. The difficulties increase in fluorescent light.

Psychologist Helen Irlen has identified a perceptual dysfunction, now known as Irlen Syndrome, caused by sensitivity to brightness and glare. She believes that half of the students with dyslexia have this difficulty.

Many students appear to be helped by modifying the light that enters the eye with coloured sheets of plastic or specially developed coloured lenses. The exact colour of the plastic or lens is determined for each person by a trained Irlen screener, usually a psychologist or special educator.

Students who have used the plastic sheets report the elimination of distortions, the ability to sustain attention for longer periods of time, increased reading rates, improved comprehension, and reduction in headaches, fatigue and other symptoms related to eye strain. See the *Studies, Surveys and Statistics* chapter for documentation of some of these results.

Clearly, adults who have difficulty picking up visual information from words, fail to get a clear image of individual letters and their position in the word, or who have difficulty monitoring their own written work because of visual distortions, would have difficulty reading and spelling.

Irlen first presented her study in 1983 to the American Psychological Association. Olive Meares, a New Zealand remedial reading teacher, made similar observations in 1980 in the educational journal, *Visible Language.* Initially Irlen's ideas were not accepted. However, subsequent studies in both Australia and the United States confirmed Irlen's observations, and her ideas are now widely accepted by psychologists and educators who work in the field of learning disabilities.

If you have a student who seems to have visual problems, recommend that she visit an opthamologist or an optometrist for a thorough examination to rule out any convergence abnormalities, refractive errors or intraocular pathology. If none of these problems exists, or if they have been corrected and visual problems persist, it may be useful to have the student tested for sensitivity to brightness. There are now Irlen screeners in most Canadian cities. The tinted glasses and coloured overlays are available only from a trained Irlen diagnostician.

For more information regarding Irlen screeners in your area, or the location of an Irlen clinic, write or call the Irlen Centre. See Appendix G for the address.

Chapter 9

Technology and Learning Disabilities

Technology and Learning Disabilities

The Computer

Using a word-processing program to write and edit on a computer has proven to be an overwhelmingly successful and welcome technique in the business and academic worlds. It has also been an excellent motivator for children with learning disabilities, and has been used successfully with adult literacy students.

At the RECLAIM Learning Centre, which houses thirty computers, we have found the computer to be an excellent motivator for our students. While using the word processor for writing, our students' spelling seems to have improved and their stories seem to be longer. Reluctant writers have been coaxed to write on the computer and have been pleased with the final product, which is neater and more legible than their own writing. The spell checker, which generates a list of possible words when an error is made, forces students to look closely at the details of words and choose the right one, thus sharpening their spelling abilities. The ease of editing cannot be emphasized strongly enough: words, phrases and sentences can be added, deleted and moved with ease. The overall result is a newfound sense of confidence when writing.

One literacy program makes maximum use of the computer. The up-to-date Ottawa Learning Centre has many computers in its impressive quarters on Rideau Street in Ottawa. The staff has researched computer software markets, developed their own software and experimented with new hardware. If you would like some advice on buying computers and programs, they would probably be glad to help you. See Appendix G for their address. See Appendix E for more information on computers and computer software.

When writing on the computer, emphasis should be on communication first and foremost. The student should be taught that the value of writing is communication. Only then should the mechanical aspects, e.g. spelling and punctuation, be taught. Many adults are slow to understand that the main purpose of writing is to communicate their ideas. Instead, they focus on spelling and other mechanical problems and get hung up on the mechanics. Once the idea of communication is firmly established and the adult is writing purposefully, you can provide a checklist of mechanical aspects to check for during the refining process.

The ease of writing, correcting and producing a final printout on the computer is attractive to the literacy student with learning disabilities. No more messy pages, erasures, crossing out or tearing out of pages! All corrections are made on the screen, with just a few simple key strokes. The printed copy looks more professional, and certainly more impressive, than the handwriting of most students. The excitement of working with modern technology is a motivating factor as well. What adult can resist saying, "I'm going to my computer class," as opposed to a reading class?

Students can and should be taught to use various invaluable features of word-processing programs. Particularly helpful to literacy students are the thesaurus and spell check features. If the student does not have access to a computer, a hand-held spell checker can be used (see Appendix E).

Ultimately, the sophisticated computer-literate student may want to be responsible for producing a student newsletter for the reading council. All it takes is willing contributors, a simple desktop publishing program and a tutor advisor. One of the most successful projects at RECLAIM's Learning Centre is the student newsletter, *Insights*.

The excitement of learning how to use the computer can be two-fold as the tutor who is unfamiliar with the computer learns along with the student and acts as an adult learning model for the student, dispelling the notion that everything has to be learned in childhood. The tutor can share her learning experiences with the student, such as how she learned best, what learning style worked for her, how she discovered new things about the computer, and how she taught herself what she wanted to know about the computer. The sheer joy of unlocking the secrets of technology together can be very exciting, and may even motivate the student as he has never been motivated before.

Regular practice in writing helps reading as well. Writing makes students come to grips with significant details of the language. Writing on the computer, which is experiential and active, can also enhance a student's reading abilities.

While the computer is recommended *mainly* as a tool for writing, it can have other uses as well. Practice can be given in various skills; educational programs for children abound, and many are appropriate for adults as well. Programs appropriate for adults are now coming on to the market at a steady pace. Phonics programs and grammar programs, for instance, are readily available. Initially, they can be quite exciting for the student, but eventually his interest may wane as his fascination with the computer wears off and the computer exercises become simply another workbook, this time on screen. On the other hand, writing on the screen is unbeatable, as any professional writer or secretary will tell you. Anyone who uses word-processing will swear the computer is the next best invention to the dishwasher—or perhaps even better.

The computer has other features. Typing on the computer keyboard is taught with the help of tutorial programs. A student can teach himself to type using the suggested practices. Computer games that promote thinking and reasoning skills are also of value, but check them out carefully before you buy them. See Appendix E for software suggestions.

The student's ability to work independently in a non-threatening environment where he is able to take risks is an added advantage of using the computer. Certainly, the novelty of using a computer should be used to its fullest advantage. Finally, it should stimulate the student and increase his confidence.

It is advisable for councils to explore the idea of buying computers and making them available for student/tutor use. If your council does not have a computer, arrange for instruction and reserve time on the computer at your local library. It's guaranteed to spice up your lessons.

Here's another suggestion. Many businesses are willing to donate so-called obsolete computers and software to literacy groups. The RECLAIM Learning Centre has many computers like these, which have been donated. Although they are not state of the art, they are extremely useful tools that suit our students' needs. Seek out companies in your area that would be willing to donate computers to your council. With a little luck, I'm sure you will be successful in finding hardware and software in a relatively short period of time.

Magnum

Magnum is a speech-driven personal assistant for the student who needs to keep an agenda, collect phone numbers and addresses, take class notes and keep reminders. Learning disabilities can make keeping track of these things very difficult. One solution is the *Magnum* recorder which was developed by *Arkenstone* and *VisuAide*.

With a traditional tape recorder, speech is recorded sequentially, making things difficult to retrieve. But with *Magnum*, speech is recorded and stored digitally on a computer disk, allowing the student to organize recordings by subject, date, name, or any other method he wishes. He will be able to find entries quickly and easily, without listening to hours of messages.

With *Magnum*'s automatic table of contents, the student can find the entry he wants, then skip directly to it. *Magnum*'s convenient marker feature allows him to place an unlimited number of markers at selected locations in entries.

Because *Magnum* records digitally, the student can insert new speech without erasing information that's already recorded, erase speech without losing any space, and cut and paste speech blocks.

Magnum has standard tape recorder keys: play, record, stop, fast forward and rewind, making it familiar and easy to learn. For more advanced functions the student can use *Magnum*'s keypad which is similar to a standard telephone keypad.

Magnum's applications feature an address book, agenda, calculator, and clock, making *Magnum* a speech-driven personal assistant. It comes with a carrying bag, a start-up disk, a manual in *Magnum* format and in print, training tapes, and a quick reference card. The *Magnum* is worthwhile investigating for students who are unable to deal with print.

For more information, contact *VisuAide*. See Appendix G for the address.

Betacom

Betacom develops and markets products that enhance the quality of life for people with disabilities. Its products and services are meant to minimize an individual's differences and help him to compete on an even playing field.

Schools, colleges and universities in Canada are struggling to meet the needs of increasing numbers of students who are reporting learning disabilities. To that end, at a recent conference on learning disabilities, *Betacom* demonstrated relevant adaptive and compensatory technologies designed to support the student with a learning disability.

Here's a short list of *Betacom* products that are useful for people with learning disabilities.

~ **Write: Outloud** This award-winning word processor reads text out loud as students write.

~ **Writing With Symbols** This is a talking word processor with a picture spell checker.

~ **The Franklin Language Master** is a portable, easy to use, talking dictionary. Users can see and hear more than 300,000 definitions and 500,000 synonyms. Words are visually highlighted to make reading easier. Words can be spelled or spoken, sound by sound. It also contains a thesaurus, spell checker, grammar help, and word games which assist learning.

~ *Betacom* also produces **VisAble**, a talking calculator with basic, scientific and statistical functions. It provides verbal reinforcement of calculations and results that appear on the visual display.

For *Betacom*'s address, see Appendix G. There are other products suitable for students with learning disabilities.

Voice-actuated Software

Dictation software is now available. Once only a futuristic idea in the realm of science fiction, voice-actuated software allows the user to dictate to the computer, which in turn creates the text. For the student with poor writing skills, this seems like a dream come true: a personal secretary. This product is now affordable and quite accurate. Encourage your student to investigate it, if it could help him. Check all suppliers in Appendix G constantly to see what's new on the market.

Chapter 10

Compensatory Strategies

Compensatory Strategies

As a child, British actress Susan Hampshire dreaded reading Shakespeare out loud in class, and went to extremes to get out of it. Once she pulled a baby hamster out of her pocket when it was her turn to read and allowed it to feed on grains on her desk. When she actually got down to reading her lines, she compensated by ad-libbing a great deal. Evasive tactics can work for some time but ultimately students have to learn to overcome their difficulties or to compensate for them.

Compensatory strategies are of utmost importance for the student with learning disabilities. Ways *must* be found to get around the student's inabilities. If the student is bright but hampered by reading, writing and spelling problems, means must be found to carry out day-to-day functions on the job or in class. Strategies include books-on-tape, dictionaries, memory aids, electronic devices, and a willingness to ask for help from other people when required.

Taped books are inexpensive and readily available to print-handicapped students. As a compensatory strategy, tapes help the slow reader to cover reading material he could not cover on his own due to time limitations. Listening to a taped book also makes the text familiar to the student and therefore easier to read. Taped books may be "read" for pleasure or to cover course work in high school or college. Books-on-tape can be borrowed from associations for the blind, or ordered from adult basic education publishers. Some libraries now carry books-on-tape. There are now approximately 80,000 titles available from Recordings for the Blind and Dyslexic. See Appendix G for their Internet address.

Adults with memory problems have to make a concerted effort to remember things, in social as well as academic situations. There is no magic solution. To remember the name of someone he has just met at a party, a student may have to repeat the name over and over again in his mind. He may even have to associate the name with something else. Mnemonic rhymes, acronyms and riddles can help students who have trouble remembering important information. An excellent source of these memory aids is Dr. Golick's book, *Playing With Words* available from Pembrooke Publishers. To remember the difficult spelling of "should", "would" and "could", for example, Dr. Golick calls them the Oh yoU Little Devil (OULD) words.

One successful dyslexic college student told me he relied heavily on the dictionary, looking up every fifth or tenth word. He had learned not to be a victim of his disability, but to take control. He also made sure he never had to read out loud, even asking his minister not to call on him to read the lesson in church.

Technology is terrific! There is the electronic pocket memory aid that can be programmed with useful text information, such as memos, appointments, phone numbers, etc. It is now quite inexpensive. Students can also revert to the low-tech version— pencil and pocket notebook.

The *Magnum* recorder is another sophisticated electronic device. It is useful for recording verbal information. See the chapter entitled *Technology and Learning Disabilities* for more information on *Magnum*.

For some students, printing is easier than cursive writing; for others, cursive writing is easier than printing. If one way is easier than the other, encourage the student to use whichever form of writing suits him best. If both are too difficult, the student should type. The computer is, of course, a natural here. As long as the student writes, it shouldn't matter how he writes.

See the chapter on *Learning Disabilities and Technology* and Appendix E for descriptions of other electronic aids that students can use to compensate for their learning disabilities. Spell checkers, grammar checkers and electronic dictionaries are examples of things that help adults compensate for poor writing skills.

Adults who use compensatory strategies often look upon them as cheating. Reinforce the idea that these strategies are fair game in learning. The most successful adult with learning disabilities I have ever met used compensatory strategies to their fullest. She had family members read and write her through college. When she graduated, she found a professional position, but was so fearful of producing written reports for her job that she came to our council for writing instruction. After two years with an extremely dedicated tutor, she has made tremendous strides by following a highly structured program.

Math Strategies

Some educators recognize learning disabilities early on and deal with them adequately. One young woman had math difficulties as a child because she couldn't remember number facts. She was told by her high school principal to use a calculator and thus get on with the business of doing her math. Eventually she showed a real talent for math and became an architect.

A simple technique can help poor math students whose work appears careless and messy, making it difficult to perform calculations properly. They simply perform all calculations on graph paper, keeping the numbers in columns. Careless errors are significantly reduced.

Talking calculators help students who learn auditorily. While performing simple addition and subtraction exercises they will learn their number facts auditorily. While doing multiplication exercises they will learn and reinforce the time tables.

Chapter 11

Accommodations

Accommodations

Colleges and universities have taken an interest in adults with learning disabilities, and are often willing to provide for their needs. Special programs with built-in support and support groups have been started at many institutions of higher education. Classroom accommodations such as untimed tests, textbooks on tape for dyslexic students, readers, assigned note-takers, word-processing courses, computers, etc. have been made available to these students.

One effective accommodation that some schools were slow to use is untimed tests. If the student gets there in the end, how long it takes should not matter. The College Entrance Examination Board, and medical and law schools are now offering untimed, sometimes oral, tests for students with certain learning disabilities.

Some schools offer extensive accommodations. They have put together programs that also include special study-skills classes and individual tutoring. If you are steering your student to a junior college or university, speak to the counsellors there to make sure your student's needs will be met.

In any educational setting, taped lectures, calculators, word processors with spelling checkers and grammar checkers, and extra time to complete exams are all fair accommodations for the student with learning disabilities. Other considerations might include making information available in both oral and written form, and giving students a distraction-free environment for studying and writing exams.

Adult literacy students, like high school or college students, need to know what they will be taught and what the tutor's expectations are. A course outline and any grading process that might be used should be given to the student in writing.

While it is unlikely that literacy students will use all of the above accommodations (appropriate for college students), many of them are of value (e.g. dictionaries, spell checkers, calculators, untimed tests, word processors and books-on-tape).

Further recommendations include speaking directly to the student; using gestures and natural expressions to convey meaning; thoroughly presenting new or technical vocabulary; relating new materials to everyday life; and providing adequate opportunities for questions and review.

When a teacher or tutor provides the students with these things, some of the techniques may become compensatory strategies, integral to the student's learning process.

Again, reiterate to the student that accommodations are not synonymous with lower standards, nor are they cheating. Encourage your student to consider them as resources.

Chapter 12

Studies, Surveys and Statistics

Studies, Surveys and Statistics

There is research literature that touches on every aspect of learning disabilities in children and adults: causes, prevalence, identification, teaching techniques, related problems, outcomes, brain-behaviour relationships, etc. These can be found in professional journals of psychology, medicine and education, and in literacy and learning disability newsletters. Reports of the most interest to the general public can be found in the popular press. What follows are some reports that I have found to be interesting and relevant, and might be of interest to literacy tutors.

Statistics on Learning Disabilities

According to a 1989 Mykebust study, it is estimated that 40% of students enrolled in literacy programs have learning disabilities. Because learning disabilities, like illiteracy, are a hidden problem, it is difficult to estimate the exact number of individuals who suffer from learning disabilities.

Irlen Study

The following is a study of the prevalence of Irlen Syndrome in an adult literacy class. Robert Ledoux, who worked for the Adult Education Services at the former Western Quebec School Board, submitted the results of a study he conducted to the *Tint Express* (the Irlen Centre newsletter).

"The group was composed of 10 males and 6 females, ranging in age from 18 to 48 years of age. Fifteen of the study group participants had recent eye examinations; only two had regular reading glasses, and everyone else had 20/20 vision. Ledoux went through a list of difficulties and distortions usually experienced by Irlen Syndrome students, including sore eyes, headaches, seeing blurry text, feelings of nausea. He recorded the number of students who reported experiencing these symptoms, as well as others.

"He then let the students experience reading with coloured overlays and recorded the improvement they felt in reading comfort. For example, one student, without an overlay could read for five minutes before experiencing reading discomfort; with the overlay, the student said he could read comfortably for approximately half an hour.

"Ledoux submitted some of the study group's comments. Below are the comments of one 18-year-old male:

"I can't read very well because it hurts. If I try to read for 15 minutes, my eyes feel like they are going to pop out of my head. I hate that! The white is too bright, the light is too bright. My eyes hurt and I often get headaches. I always wear a cap in class and I turn my book away from the window. When I try to read, the page gets blurry and the words move and rise one or two inches above the paper. I can see each letter and its grey shadow down below it. Everything seems to vibrate. Sometimes I have to use my finger so I won't lose my place. I try to read, but I don't understand or remember what I have just read. It is very frustrating! Now, I have two coloured overlays, a pink and a green. I use them all the time. I don't read much faster, and I still make mistakes, but at least the words don't move, float, or vibrate any more!

I read for one and a half hours the other day, and my eyes did not pop out. I did not even get a headache. This is great!"

"Ledoux pointed out that during his interview with the above participant, he offered him the choice between a class in which he could work at a ratio of three students per teacher and give up the new overlays, or keep the overlays and not have the reduced student/teacher ratio. The 18-year-old was quick to decline the offer. With the overlay, he felt he could do most of the work himself.

"Ledoux concluded that before school boards invest more time and money in tutoring a weak reader, they should make sure that he or she sees the printed page the way it is meant to appear. He reiterates that the overlays are a very effective and inexpensive tool, and that the Irlen Syndrome, unlike many learning disabilities, is relatively simple to identify."

OBSERVATIONS REPORTED

Robert Ledoux observed that eleven of the subjects that he had observed read comfortably for much longer periods of time when they used coloured overlays. Three other students with severe reading disabilities were not evaluated by this criteria.

Minutes of Comfortable Reading Without Overlays	Minutes of Comfortable Reading With Overlays	Number of Students
5	25-40	3
10	30-90	2
15	60	3
15	90	1
30	120	1
60	60	1

See Appendix G for the address of the Irlen Centre in Ottawa.

Speaking for Themselves

In the Spring 1992 *Adult Literacy, What Does the Research Say?* newsletter, Dr. Margie Golick reported on the following study of individuals with learning disabilities.

"Frustration, depression, feeling dumb. Determination, struggle, supportive families, sense of humour. Persistent difficulties with reading, writing and direction. These are some of the recurrent themes in adults' accounts of their lives with learning disabilities.

"In a much-needed piece of qualitative research, psychologists Paul Gerber and Henry Reiff invited nine adults with a history of severe school difficulties to give us a look at learning disabilities from an insider's point of view. They report their study in *Speaking for*

Themselves, a [1991] monograph sponsored by the International Academy for Research in Learning Disabilities, published by the University of Michigan Press.

"There were six men and three women in the study, their ages ranging from 22 to 56. For purposes of analysis, they were divided into three groups based on educational and vocational achievements. Through a series of detailed interviews, the investigators explored educational experiences and looked at vocational achievements, social-emotional adjustment and adaptations to daily life.

"Not surprisingly, there was wide variation in the achievements and adaptations of the nine, with more similarities within each of the groups than across groups. Yet all report strikingly similar experiences resulting from their early inabilities to learn basic skills at school—embarrassment, frustration, teasing, and a poor self-image. Some were misclassified as mentally retarded and, even as little children, had to convince the people around them that they did not belong in classes for students with profound developmental delays. Each was eventually diagnosed as having learning disabilities, but this did not always result in appropriate class placements.

"*Speaking for Themselves* brings both good news and bad news. The bad news is that cognitive difficulties persist in people with learning disabilities. The good news is that many lead fulfilling lives despite their problem.

"Many of the adults who approach literacy centres for help tell similar stories: frustration at school, repeated experiences of educational and vocational failure, and fuzzy or unrealistic goals. Despite unanswered questions, *Speaking for Themselves* highlights some of the essential needs of these adults. Along with instruction in the three R's, they need a sympathetic response, a chance to be successful in a learning situation, help in understanding their strengths and weaknesses, help in formulating goals, and guidance on the pathways to achieving those goals."

Statistics Canada Survey

The 1989 Statistics Canada literacy survey shows (using graphs) lower levels of literacy attained by adults with learning disabilities, compared to the overall group surveyed. The reading levels are described as follows:

LEVEL 1 Difficulty dealing with printed materials; identify themselves as non-readers;

LEVEL 2 Can use printed materials for limited purposes only such as finding a familiar word in a simple text;

LEVEL 3 Can use reading materials in a variety of situations if material is simple and clearly laid out and tasks involved are simple; functional literacy;

LEVEL 4 Can meet most everyday reading demands; full literacy.

Students who stated that they had a learning disability at one time, had one at the present time, or had been in a special class for students with learning difficulties tested as follows compared to the general population: a higher percentage of the students with learning disabilities/difficulties read at levels one and two, and a lower percentage of them read at level four.

Teaching Reading to Adults with Learning Disabilities

The following are excerpts from an article entitled "Teaching Reading to Adults with Learning Disabilities" by Dr. Margie Golick. It appeared in the Spring 1991 issue of *Adult Literacy, What Does the Research Say?*

"In an extensive review of the educational, psychological and linguistical research, psychologist Marilyn Adams summarizes the results of more than 600 studies that have implications for the teaching of reading. Although most of these studies were conducted with children, there seem to be general principles that apply to the teaching of reading to students of any age.

1   For effective reading, it is necessary to establish the alphabetic principle—that words are composed of sounds in sequence, and that letters and groups of letters represent these sounds in an ordered, left-to-right way.

2   In a large series of studies that compared different approaches to the teaching of reading, it was clearly demonstrated that the most successful ones included systematic phonics instruction.

3   Among these, the most successful were those that offered, along with the explicit teaching of the decoding of words, plenty of opportunity for meaningful reading of connected text. It is not a question of phonics or whole language, but phonics and a rich experience with meaningful language that makes a skilful reader.

4   Effective comprehension depends on word recognition skills that are effortless and automatic. This comes about through practice with words and careful attention to both a word's printed form and what it says.

"Adams summarizes the research that highlights the advantages of well-developed phonics skills.

1   Knowing how to figure out words gives beginning readers some independence in their efforts at word learning.

2   Furthermore, sounding out words focuses the students' attention on the letter patterns in words, helps them learn likely and unlikely sequences of letters, thereby reinforcing memory for spelling.

3   The ultimate result is that word recognition is more automatic.

4   While it is true that sensitivity to context and meaning facilitates the decoding process, the capacity for sounding out words, in turn, assists higher order comprehension. The auditory-image of words (even when only pronounced mentally), remain in memory longer than visual images, thus allowing the reader, reading a complex sentence, to hold on to parts of it until an interpretation can be made. This helps the reader, too, to recall details, or combine them to relate facts, or make meaningful inferences.

"Because phonics instruction means different things to different people, because programs are so diverse, Adams reviews the research to try to tease out the essential ingredients. There are, first of all, no data to support the use of different teaching methods for the auditory learner or the visual learner. To cope with an alphatic writing system, all students must first develop phonological awareness, the capacity to analyze spoken words into their component parts. Training in this awareness is helped by the following:

1. Dividing words into syllables (even clapping them out and feeling and hearing the differences in, for example, but, but-ter, but-ter-fly).

2. Rhyming activities (reading poems, producing rhymes, and hearing the similarities in rhyming words).

3. Becoming aware that before the vowel in English syllables there is a range of different kinds of "onsets", as in sing, ring, sting, string, spring, sling, swing, etc.

These are intermediary stages before:

4. Isolating and identifying beginning sounds, word final and internal sounds."

In the same article Dr. Golick stated the following:

"Literacy tutors may feel apprehensive about tackling the persistent literacy problems of someone who has had years of schooling. They should be encouraged by a finding in the long-term follow-up study of psychologist Maggie Bruck. In her study of 100 adults whose difficulties had been diagnosed in childhood, she found that even in adult life, exposure to literacy tasks resulted in continued improvement in literacy skills."

Scientists Identify Genetic Marker for Reading Disabilities

The Spring 1995 Learning Disabilities Association of Canada newsletter *National* reported the following:

"Scientists have identified a genetic basis for dyslexia in a study of people with reading disabilities. The researchers said they have narrowed their search for a dyslexia gene to a tiny region of chromosome 6. Bruce Pennington, a psychology professor at the University of Denver (Colorado) said, "What is inherited is a gene that affects some aspects of the way the brain develops. That in turn affects some aspect of language development so that it makes reading difficult.

"The scientists from four U.S. research centres, led by Lon Cardon of Stanford University, interviewed more than 450 members of families with a history of reading disabilities. The study also included 100 non-identical twins where at least one in each pair was dyslexic."

Learning Disability Discrimination

The Spring 1995 *National* reported the following:

"Individuals with learning disabilities such as dyslexia are stigmatized and often discriminated against as a result of misinformation despite the fact that 10-15% of North Americans suffer from some form of learning disability. That is one of the key conclusions of a new nationwide poll, the most comprehensive survey ever on Americans' knowledge and attitudes about learning disabilities, which was commissioned by the Emily Hall Tremaine Foundation and conducted by Roper Starch Worldwide. The poll of 1,207 adults across the United States was conducted in January 1995.

"The poll, along with additional focus group research commissioned by the Tremaine Foundation, reveals a serious lack of public awareness of learning disabilities.

"Among the poll's findings:

~ 44% say they received 'less than equal treatment' in school because of their disabilities. Thirty-eight percent of parents of children with learning disabilities believe their children receive less than equal treatment because of their disabilities.

~ 85% of Americans agree that children with learning disabilities are often put down by teachers and fellow students at school.

~ More than 6 in 10 (65%) believe adults who have learning disabilities are sometimes fired when their learning disabilities become public.

~ A shocking 33% believe people with learning disabilities 'are sometimes not safe to be around in the workplace'.

"When initially questioned about learning disabilities, between 60-85% incorrectly identified a number of conditions as being associated with learning disabilities, including mental retardation, blindness and emotional problems."

U.S.A. Statistics

The Spring 1996 *National* reported these statistics:

"Although these statistics do not accurately reflect the Canadian learning disabilities situation, many Canadian researchers feel that some of these numbers are not far off the Canadian mark.

~ 75-80% of special education students identified with learning disabilities have their basic deficits in language and reading *(Source: National Institute of Health)*.

~ 60% of adults with severe literacy problems have undetected or untreated learning disabilities *(Source: National Adult Literacy and Learning Disabilities Centre, 1994)*.

~ 50% of juvenile delinquents tested were found to have undetected learning disabilities *(Source: National Centre for State Courts and the Educational Testing Service, 1977)*.

~ Up to 60% of adolescents in treatment for substance abuse have learning disabilities *(Source: Hazelden Foundation, Minnesota, 1992)*.

~ 62% of students with learning disabilities were unemployed one year after graduation *(Source: National Longitudinal Transition Study, 1991)*."

Chapter 13

The Devil's Advocate

The Devil's Advocate

Many people, including professionals, have taken exception to the concept of learning disabilities, maintaining that it is a middle class phenomenon—a euphemism used to describe slow learners, or even the mentally retarded. Others have claimed that the disabilities are only differences, not neurological abnormalities—simply differences that can be found between any two groups of people.

However, neurologists and psychologists have now determined that learning disabilities do exist and in fact, there is a neurological basis for learning disabilities.

From my experience as a literacy practitioner, I can say with certainty that there is evidence of a group of learners distinct from slow learners. Slow learners are slow at all aspects of learning. These others are often bright, confident, and capable of complex thought. They have accomplished more academically and know exactly what their needs are, as opposed to slow learners, who come to us with the vague notion of improving their education. The needs of students with learning disabilities are usually quite similar: they want to improve their spelling and writing to more adult-like levels, as well as improve their weak decoding skills. Many of them aspire to higher education.

Some people say that there are no learning disabilities, only teaching disabilities. The media has seized this convenient scapegoat to explain the large numbers of students who write poorly and spell abominably. While there may be some truth to the popular theory that writing standards have plummeted since the 1960s, when content was emphasized over mechanics, we cannot blame poor spatial orientation and attention deficits on the '60s.

Conclusion

In light of the impact illiteracy has on this country, ranging from curtailing access to basic human rights to the enormous cost to Canadian business, and bearing in mind that learning disabilities are at least partially responsible for adult illiteracy, governments should clearly be concerned about the issue. Generally speaking, the people we are concerned with and the people we label as adults with learning disabilities are of average or above average intelligence. No words are strong enough to express the tragedy of losing the potentially valuable contribution of this segment of society.

Adequate funding is needed to develop tools to identify and assess adults with learning disabilities. A battery of assessment tools and techniques still needs to be developed by psychologists specializing in learning disabilities in conjunction with experienced literacy personnel. Research on remediation and compensatory strategies needs attention as well.

As a federal government discussion paper on literacy suggests, good awareness programs should help remove the stigma of being illiterate. Those same programs should explain what learning disabilities are, drawing analogies to physical disabilities and emphasizing learners' intelligence.

A further recommendation is for everyone who works in the field of literacy to develop an awareness of how learning disabilities affect literacy. With a better understanding of learning disabilities, some tools for diagnosis and assessment, and some knowledge of remediation and assistance techniques, you should now have the confidence to address your student's needs.

Of course, there will be times when you need the help of a professional. Do not hesitate to ask for help when you need it. Essentially, after a thorough student evaluation, trial and error is required to see which techniques or combination of techniques work best with each student. The key is knowing your student and his needs, as well as his style of learning.

The "teach to the ability/teach to the disability" dialogue still rages. Again, there is no firm answer. There is no panacea. Each case must be treated individually. Use your judgement. You know the student best. If the tutor requires guidance, she should speak to the co-ordinator, who may herself require advice from a learning disabilities professional or association in your area.

The Learning Disabilities Association of Canada's position paper on learning disabilities supports the idea that literacy programs must become involved:

"…that all literacy programs provide comprehensive training for service providers to ensure effective educational service for people with learning disabilities."

Recommendations For Literacy Providers

~ Educate literacy professionals in your organization on learning disabilities. Publish a summary of this guide in your newsletter. Distribute this guide to those who may have students with learning disabilities.

~ Enlist the help of your local learning disabilities association or experts in the field of learning disabilities.

~ Organize an in-service workshop on learning disabilities.

~ Evaluate the student in an in-depth interview (see Appendix D).

~ Use the assessment tools/techniques found in this book.

~ Identify students with learning disabilities.

~ Assess each student's strengths and weaknesses.

~ Explain to the student where his strengths, weaknesses and abilities lie, demystifying the problem of learning disabilities. In other words, motivate the student.

~ Prepare an individualized program for each student, based on his interests, goals and needs.

~ Provide remedial support in the areas where skills are weak, in as sequential a fashion as possible.

~ Teach the student to use his strengths and the learning style that suits him best.

~ Teach the student to compensate for or get accommodation for his disabilities.

~ Give support and/or refer the student to a support group.

~ Monitor the student's progress; nothing succeeds like success!

~ Debunk the notion that the literacy student or student with learning disabilities is stupid. Organize a public awareness campaign. Distribute fliers.

Although learning disabilities are permanent, students do learn how to read, write and spell better; however, spelling problems seem to persist. Teach your student to depend on a dictionary, hand-held spelling checker or, if he is lucky enough to have access to one, a computer. Spelling need never hold him hostage again.

It has been stated by many educators, including Dr. Golick, and my own literacy experience bears this out, that there are some learners who simply cannot learn what you would like them to learn. Despite the best teaching efforts, some do not become functional; some don't even learn to read beyond a grade two level. In the most difficult cases, I recommend that the tutor teach only emergency words and life skills. While such students often become *more* functional, they do not achieve a grade nine reading level.

Successful students use their intact channels, and are highly motivated—even tenacious. Tom Cruise is an example of such determination. His acting success, he claims, is the result of drive and steadfastness that goes back to his childhood battle with dyslexia. He learned early in life to set goals for himself and be disciplined to overcome the barriers and shame of being in a remedial class. Like so many other successful kids with learning disabilities, he had an aware and equally determined parent working on his behalf. His mother, who had studied special education, recognized his problems and provided tutoring and motivation. His mother said, "Look, you're dyslexic, so you'll just have to work harder at what others take for granted," Cruise told a reporter. He apparently accepted her help and advice, and by junior high school had managed to get himself out of the remedial class he had been in since kindergarten. [You, as the tutor, may have to advocate for and motivate your student, just as parents of successful children have done.] Cruise says it was his childhood battle that prepared him for his eight-year drive to stardom.

Encourage tenacious students like Cruise to "go for it". Students with tenacity are the most likely to succeed.

Others have succeeded because they have natural verbal ability. They bring a richness of experience to the page because they have a good understanding of language, and they use their language skills to make their living. A number of prominent politicians, actors and writers have written or talked publicly about their dyslexia. If your student has excellent verbal skills, teach her to use them appropriately, perhaps at a job where these skills will ensure her success.

People with success stories report that they may read a great deal, but they often remain slow readers and poor spellers. What is the ultimate compensatory strategy for the very successful adult with learning disabilities? I've heard it and seen it time and time again: they get good secretaries!

One thing that most educators agree upon is that the field of learning disabilities is new and constantly evolving, and that no one yet has all the answers. Therefore I urge you to keep reading about developments in the field, and apply them to your student. Like your student, you too will be learning!

Bibliography

Adult Literacy, What Does the Research Say? RECLAIM; Spring 1991.

Ibid., Spring 1992.

ALBSU Specific Learning Disabilities. No. 32, Winter 1989; Adult Literacy Basic Skills Unit; London, England.

Bringing Literacy Within Reach: Identifying Adults with Learning Disabilities: Learning Disabilities Association of Canada; 1991.

The Gazette. January 8, 1989; Montreal, Canada.

Golick, Margie, Ph.D. *Learning Disabilities in Post-Secondary Education.* Report on the Maritime Provinces Higher Education Commission; December 1988.

Hampshire, Susan. *Susan's Story.* St. Martin's Press, N.Y.; 1982.

Learning Disabilities and Literacy. Learning Disabilities Association of Ontario; undated.

Loring, C. Brinckerhoff, Address at the *Learning Disabilities Conference.* University of Montreal; August 22, 1996.

National. Learning Disabilities Association of Canada; Vol. XXIV, No. 8; Spring 1988.

Ibid., Winter 1994, Vol. XXI, No. 3.

Ibid., Spring 1995, Vol. XXXI, No. 4.

Ibid., Winter 1995, Vol. XXXII, No. 3.

Ibid., Spring 1996, Vol. XXXII, No. 4.

Ibid., Summer 1996, Vol. XXXIII, No. 1.

Psychology Today. February, 1986.

Savage, John F. *Dyslexia, Understanding Reading Problems.*
Julian Messner, N.Y.; 1985.

Smith, Bert Kruger. *Dilemma of A Dyslexic Man.* The Hogg
Foundation for Mental Health; The University of Texas; 1968.

Specific Learning Disabilities in the Adult Years. ACLD, Inc.;
Pittsburgh, PA; undated.

The Tint Express. Irlen Syndrome Canadian Information and
Support Group; Kars, Ontario, Canada.

APPENDIX A

Definitions of Learning Disabilities

The following official definition of learning disabilities was adopted by the Canadian Association for Children and Adults with Learning Disabilities (now Learning Disabilities Association of Canada) on October 18, 1981:

Learning disabilities is a generic term that refers to a heterogeneous group of disorders due to identifiable or inferred central nervous system dysfunction. Such disorders may be manifested by delays in early development and/or difficulties in any of the following areas: attention, memory, reasoning, coordination, communicating, reading, writing, spelling, calculation, social competence and emotional maturation.

Learning disabilities are intrinsic to the individual and may affect learning and behaviour in any individual, including those with potentially average, average or above average intelligence.

Learning disabilities are not due primarily to visual, hearing, or motor handicaps; to mental retardation, emotional disturbance, or environmental disadvantage; although they may occur concurrently with any of these.

Learning disabilities may arise from genetic variations, biochemical factors, events in the pre- to perinatal period, or any other subsequent events resulting in neurological impairment.

The following definition of learning disabilities was adopted by the U.S. National Joint Committee on Learning Disabilities, 1988:

"Learning disabilities" is a general term that refers to a heterogeneous group of disorders manifested by significant difficulties in the acquisition and use of listening, speaking, reading, writing, reasoning or mathematical abilities. These disorders are intrinsic to the individual, presumed to be due to central nervous system dysfunction, and may occur across the life span. Problems in self-regulatory behaviours, social perception and social interaction may exist with learning disabilities but do not by themselves constitute a learning disability. Although learning disabilities may occur concomitantly with other handicapping conditions (e.g. sensory impairment, mental retardation, serious emotional disturbance) or with extrinsic influences (e.g. cultural differences, insufficient or inappropriate instruction), they are not the result of those conditions or influences.

Learning Disabilities Associations in Canada

Learning Disabilities Association of Canada

National Office
323 Chapel Street
Ottawa, Ont., K1N 7Z2
Tel. (613) 238-5721

LDA ALBERTA

145-11343-61st Avenue
Edmonton, Alta., T6H 1M3
Tel. (403) 448-0360

LDA BRITISH COLUMBIA

204-3402-27th Avenue
Vernon, B.C., V1T 1S1
Tel. (250) 524-5033

LDA MANITOBA

60 Maryland St., 2nd Floor
Winnipeg, Man., R3G 1K7
Tel. (204) 774-1821

LDA NEW BRUNSWICK

420 York Street
Fredericton, N.B., E3B 3P7
Tel. (506) 459-7852

LDA NORTHWEST TERRITORIES

P.O. Box 242
Yellowknife, N.W.T., X1A 2N2
Tel. (403) 873-6378

LDA NOVA SCOTIA

1800 Argyle Street, Suite 517
Halifax, N.S., B3T 3N8
Tel. (902) 464-9751

LDA ONTARIO

365 Bloor Street E.,
Box 39, Suite 1004
Toronto, Ont., M4W 3L4
Tel. (416) 929-4311

LDA QUEBEC (AQETA)

300-284 Notre Dame Street W.
Montreal, Que., H2Y 1T7
Tel. (514) 847-1324

LDA SASKATCHEWAN

Albert Community Centre
912 Ildywyld Drive
Saskatoon, Sask., S7L 0Z6
Tel. (306) 652-4114

LDA YUKON TERRITORY

P.O. Box 4853
Whitehorse, Yukon, Y1A 4N6
Tel. (403) 668-5167

APPENDIX C
Outline for a Learning Disabilities Workshop

An in-service workshop for tutors on learning disabilities is a must. The two workshops Dr. Golick gave to our tutors were extremely well received. An entire workshop was devoted to identifying and determining student problems. The second dealt with remediation. If you can find a qualified professional to deliver a workshop to your council, by all means do so. If you are unable to obtain help from your local university or learning disabilities association (see Appendix B for addresses and phone numbers), enhance your own knowledge about learning disabilities by reading as much as you can, and by speaking to as many knowledgeable people as you can; then develop a workshop with your council. What follows is a suggested outline for a learning disabilities workshop.

Introductions

ICEBREAKER Ask each participant to complete this statement: "If I had a learning disability, it would be…" Explain that what each of the participants has identified is most likely a learning difference, and that a learning disability is a more exaggerated version.

OBJECTIVES Ask participants what their objectives are for the workshop. List them on a blackboard or flip chart. Make sure their needs are met at some point.

DEFINITION Literacy tutors prefer participatory workshops. Ask them to brainstorm to arrive at a definition of learning disabilities. Write it on a flip chart or blackboard. Then present the official definitions (photocopied handouts).

THE STUDENT   What does he look like? How does she act? Elicit student characteristics from tutors. Fill in the characteristics that do not come up. Ask tutors if they have ever had students who fit the description of a student with learning disabilities. Ask the tutors to describe those students. Relate the names and careers of famous people who had/have learning disabilities. Discuss.

VIDEO   Show the video *How Difficult Can This Be?*. It is an excellent video on the subject of learning disabilities. This unique video allows viewers to experience the same frustration, anxiety and tension that children with learning disabilities face in their daily lives. A series of striking simulations helps those of us who work with adults with learning disabilities to better understand them. The video can be ordered from the Visual Education Centre. See Appendix G for the address.

ASSESSMENT   Talk about assessment techniques and how they are linked to remediation. Role play using the diagnostic tool entitled *Interview Format and Questionnaire* found in Appendix D.

REMEDIATION   Talk about remediation techniques.

COMPENSATORY STRATEGIES   Talk about compensatory strategies that students can use. What compensatory strategies have tutors used in their own learning? Discuss.

ACCOMMODATION   Talk about accommodations being used in higher education. Ask the tutors what accommodations they might use with their literacy students.

QUIZ   Use the quiz on the following page so that tutors can self-test their knowledge on learning disabilities.

CONCLUSION   What did the tutors learn? What needs to be included in the next workshop on learning disabilities?

Learning Disabilities Quiz

Test your knowledge of learning disabilities. Match the Learning Disability Characteristic with the appropriate Behavioural Description on the following page. The answers appear at the bottom of page 93.

LD Characteristics

1 Generalization _____

2 Auditory figure-ground _____

3 Critical thinking/insight _____

4 Visual discrimination _____

5 Dyslexic _____

6 Sequential logic _____

7 Vocalic communication _____

8 Visual-motor integration _____

9 Broad attention deployment _____

10 Auditory memory _____

11 Expressive language _____

12 Spatial relations _____

Behavioural Description

A Has difficulty getting ideas or feelings across to others; never seems to get to the point.

B Has problems in modelling an instructor's movement in a shop class.

C Fails to recognize supervisor's stern tone.

D Trouble organizing and planning work assignments; frequently ends up redoing work.

E Tends to reverse numbers when entering sales projection figures in the quarterly report.

F Trouble seeing fine differences in the shades of colour on litmus paper in the chemistry lab.

G Unable to detect flaws in work performance.

H Gets confused when given verbal and written directions to locate a delivery site.

I Difficulty understanding public address system in airports.

J Able to tune-in to numerous visual stimuli simultaneously.

K Has trouble applying previously learned skills to novel situations.

L When calling directory assistance, needs to have operator place the call because she can't remember it long enough to dial it.

Answers:

1-K, 2-I, 3-G, 4-F, 5-E, 6-D, 7-C, 8-B, 9-J, 10-L, 11-A, 12-H

APPENDIX D
Interview Format and Questionnaire

I have used this diagnostic tool numerous times and find that it is an excellent way to get to know a student's strengths and weaknesses. Done properly, this test takes several hours to complete. You can complete it over several sessions. I'm sure that both you and your student will find the experience fascinating.

Having completed the interview with your student, you will not be entitled to diagnose that your student has a learning disability. That we leave to the professionals. However, you will get a sense of whether your student has average or above average intelligence, and may have a learning disability, or that he has many weak areas and may be a slow learner.

The most important result will be that with your student, you will discover areas of strength and areas that need remediation. The surprising thing you will find is how sensible it all is.

Guidelines for Interviewing Adults Who May Have Learning Disabilities

Find out about...

1   **School history**

2   **Life experiences**

3   **Present status**

4   **Goals**

5 Reading: words
~ non-words (phonic analysis)
~ text material—can reading be sustained for a reasonable length of time?

6 Spelling: learned words
~ phonic awareness
~ spelling conventions
~ grammatical endings

7 Writing: handwriting (is it legible? does it come automatically?)
~ cursive writing
~ printing
~ knowledge of conventions and ability to use them

8 Language: real life situations
~ auditory processing
~ effect of background noise
~ discrimination
~ rate
~ vocabulary
~ word retrieval
~ syntax: grammar
~ sentence structure

9 Memory: immediate memory
~ long-term memory (general information about world)
~ verbal learning
~ non-verbal learning
~ learning of sequences (months, tables, etc.)

10 Visual-spatial abilities:
~ handedness
~ awareness of left and right
~ sense of direction
~ copying designs
~ life skills: building, sewing, etc.

Questionnaire

Reading

Do you find reading difficult?

What do you remember about learning to read at school?

Did you have trouble learning the alphabet? With letter names? Sounds of letters? Blending sounds? Building a sight vocabulary? Spelling words?

Do you read more slowly than other people?

Do you have trouble understanding what you read?

Do you often have to skip words because you can't figure them out? One or more per paragraph?

What happens when you read?

Do you tire easily? Do you get frustrated?

Do you take breaks? How often? What's the longest you can go without taking a break?

What happens when you get tired?

Do you ever fall asleep while reading?

Do you feel restless, fidgety, or need to get up and walk around while reading?

How do your eyes feel?

What happens to the printed page?

If you push yourself to continue, what happens?

Do you skip lines without meaning to?

Do you lose your place?

Do you like to use something—finger, ruler, etc.—to help you keep your place?

Do you leave out or insert words?

Do you misread words?

Do you have to reread to make sense of what you are reading?

What kind of light do you like to read in?

Is there a time of day when you prefer to read?

Do you feel eye strain—fatigue, tearing, dryness, pain, headaches, etc.?

Do you have trouble visualizing scenes described in a story?

Can you follow written directions?

Can you skim or speed read with comprehension?

When you move your eyes rapidly across the page, do all the words stay in focus?

Linguistic Skills Related to Reading

Are there many words you don't understand?

Do you know the meaning of frequently used connective words: like, however, although, nevertheless, therefore?

Are some sentences too complicated to disentangle?
Examples: Before you wash the dishes, sweep the floor.
The cat that the bird saw fell out of the tree.

Do you forget details by the time you reach the end of a paragraph or story?

Do you have trouble pronouncing words?

Do you find reading to yourself easier than reading aloud?

Writing and Spelling

Are you right- or left-handed?

Do you use different hands for different tasks?

Do you avoid writing?

Do you still find it an effort to form letters?

Do you prefer script or printing?

Do you sometimes mix script and printing?

Does your hand get tired?

Do you find your fingers sometimes play tricks on you and you write something that you did not intend to write? Do you write the same word twice? Leave out letters or a whole word? Substitute a word for a similar one?

Do you find it hard to proofread what you write and spot mistakes?

Math

Was math hard or easy for you in school?

Do you know or did you have a hard time learning number facts? Times tables?

If number facts are not automatic, does it help to use your fingers? Rapid counting? A calculator?

Can you add and subtract better if you write it down than by doing it in your head?

Do you have trouble hanging on to the details of a question unless everything is written down?

Do you forget procedures (say, long division) that you have not used for some time?

Do you ever make "careless" mistakes, e.g. fail to notice whether the sign is plus or minus; forget to add on a number you have "carried"; add numbers from the wrong column, etc.?

Can you do word problems if given a calculator?

Do you have trouble understanding the word problem, knowing what operation you have to do?

Does math language ever get you mixed up?
Examples: What number must be added to 346 to get 501 for the sum?
Give the number that is 269 less than the sum of 3268, 4297, and 6598.
Find the number that is three times the difference of 2003 and 867.
Find the number that is 67 more than the quotient of 1728 and 27.

Do you know your math facts but find it hard to finish timed tests?

Do you reverse numbers or write them down incorrectly?

Do you sometimes copy numbers down wrong, or write a different number from the one you intended (e.g. 42 for 24)?

Do you check your bill in a store or restaurant?

Do you have trouble making change?

Do you count your change in a store or restaurant?

Do you know how to calculate a tip?

Do you understand interest rates?

Do you know what is meant by percent?

Do you understand 50% off? Reduced by 1/3?

Do you understand fractions?

What day-to-day math gives you trouble?

Do you know or did you have trouble learning in school the meanings of frequently used words, e.g. parallel, hypotenuse, remainder, perpendicular?

Memory

Did you have trouble learning basic math facts?

Did you have trouble learning and remembering the spelling of words?

Did you have trouble learning words on flash cards?

Do you have trouble remembering people's names?

Do you have trouble learning new words—for example, words associated with a new job or skill you are learning?

Do you have trouble memorizing the words to a song or poem?

Do you sometimes have trouble figuring out what the individual words are in a song or poem?

Do you have trouble remembering phone numbers or addresses?

Do you or did you have trouble learning lists such as days of the week or months of the year?

Are you a fast forgetter?

Strengths and Learning Style

What are you good at?

~ Things you do with your hands?

~ Drawing? Other arts and crafts?

~ Repairing things?

~ Understanding how mechanical things work? Electrical things?

~ Building things?

~ Painting, wallpapering, plumbing, wiring?

~ Playing musical instruments? Singing? Appreciating music?

~ Dancing?

~ Sports—skiing, skating, hockey, ball sports, tennis, running, gymnastics, swimming?

~ Hobbies?

~ Cooking?

~ Organizing, managing?

~ Number work?

~ Words, oral expression?

~ Creating stories?

~ Understanding diagrams?

~ Understanding maps, charts, graphs?

Do you get along well with people?

Do you make friends easily?

Do people like to tell you their troubles and ask you advice?

Do you have a good sense of humour?

Are you reliable?

Are you generally punctual?

Are you persistent, sticking to something until you get it done?

Are you generally cheerful?

Compensatory Strategies

How do you remember lists, directions, etc.?

~   Verbally

~   Visually

~   Pictorially

How do you try to learn spelling words?

~   Writing words out

~   Reciting them

~   Both at the same time

Do you use rhythm, rhyme, mnemonics, movement? Describe how.

Do you use a calculator for math?

Do you have people read to you?

Do you ask someone to read words you can't read?

Do you get books on tape?

Are you a careful listener? Do you pick up information that way?

Do you get help in writing and filling out forms?

Do you dictate things to other people?

Do you use a word processor and spelling checker?

Do you ask people to repeat things to you if you didn't get it clearly the first time?

Do you repeat it back to make sure that you have it straight?

Do you ask to have directions written down?

Do you keep an agenda or appointment calendar and write down appointments, due dates, etc., to make sure you remember them?

Are you organized and systematic, so you can keep track of your things?

Do you use dictionaries?

Do you use a spelling reference book?

Do you use photography, videotaping or art that enables you to express ideas or produce information in non-verbal form?

Have you learned how to talk about your reading difficulty without feeling embarrassed?

Visual-Spatial Skills

Do you mix up 'b' and 'd'?

Do you confuse numbers, such as 24 and 42?

Do you have a poor sense of direction?

Are you easily lost in a new place?

Do you confuse left and right? On yourself? Or following directions?

Can you read maps?

~ Follow a pattern?

~ Follow directions to assemble something?

This interview format and questionnaire were prepared by Dr. Margie Golick. Tutor feedback and reports on your experiences using it will help refine and improve the questionnaire. Please send your comments to:

Dr. Margie Golick
The Learning Associates of Montreal
4203 Ste-Catherine Street West
Montreal, Quebec, H3Z 1P6

APPENDIX E
Computers And Spell Checkers

Computers

What kind of computer should your student buy? That depends on his needs and budget. To improve writing skills, an "obsolete" computer, like an IBM compatible 386 and a dot matrix printer, would even do. Students can use them to practise their writing.

At the other end of the continuum are Pentium computers which can support Windows programs and Internet. Windows programs make the computer more "user friendly". They operate more like MacIntosh computers in that they are menu-driven and use icons rather than words or function keys. The icons (small pictures) are advantageous to students who have trouble with reading. Upper level students may want to tap into the Internet or use complex software.

I have referred to IBM and IBM compatible systems because that is what I use and am familiar with. IBM compatible computers are being used in RECLAIM's Learning Centre and are the kind of computer that is most commonly donated to our Centre.

The MacIntosh may still be more user friendly, but it is also more expensive. It is an excellent computer for graphics and desktop publishing. However, in the world of business, IBM and IBM compatibles still appear to prevail.

Computer Programs

These days, computer programs can be found for almost anything, almost anywhere. They are advertised in education resource catalogues and magazines and in computer magazines found at your local drug store. They can be bought from the Internet, computer stores, Radio Shack, department stores, etc. Available in two formats (disk and CD-Rom), most are affordable but not cheap.

I highly recommend that the first investment be a word-processing program. For the office, WordPerfect and Word are practically "de rigueur". Look for something easier for the beginner. Consult the educational division of Apple or IBM, depending on which system you are using. Be sure the program you buy has a spell checker and a thesaurus. Word processing programs are the ones that students with learning disabilities will benefit from the most.

Invest in a simple typing tutor program as well. Math drills and phonic and cloze exercises might be next on your shopping list. Next, look into games, puzzles, etc. There's no end to the list of available subjects, so don't let this be the end of your list.

Investigate

Here is a list of some computer software currently in our Learning Centre on 486 computers:

GRAMMAR GREMLINS (Davidson). Tests students' knowledge and tells areas needing review (i.e., capitalization, punctuation, parts of speech). Gives immediate feedback except in the test component.

WORD ATTACK PLUS (Davidson). This software introduces new words. In this program, there is a fair amount of reading, little writing, and an activity card game, which students enjoy. There is also a multiple choice test.

MATH BLAST PLUS (Davidson). Mathematical equations and games are available for addition, subtraction, division, multiplication, fractions, decimals, and percentages. Has straight equations or video game-like activities.

ENCARTA WORLD ATLAS (Microsoft Corp.) Interactive odyssey that lets you experience the continents and countries, the sights and sounds, the cultures, the facts and figures that make up today's world.

WHERE IN THE WORLD IS CARMEN SANDIEGO? (Broderbund). An excellent program for higher level readers that focuses on developing research abilities. This program helps develop an awareness of geography.

MAVIS BEACON TEACHES TYPING (Mindscape). An excellent typing tutor for all levels.

AUTOSKILLS (Autoskill Inc.). This software was designed originally for people with learning disabilities. It is a multilevel phonics-based program that tests a variety of reading sub-skill and then provides specific remediation accordingly.

THE NEW READING DISK (Cambridge Training Development, U.K.). This is a new and exciting piece of software. It is a multimedia CD-ROM designed to help adults learn to read through writing. The New Reading Disk has features that allow the user to customize the content.

Here are numerous new programs you may wish to investigate: Compton's Interactive Encyclopedia (Compton's New Media Inc.); Bookshelf (Microsoft Corp.); Spell It Plus (Davidson); Crossword Magic (L & S Computerware); and Where in Time is Carmen Sandiego? (Broderbund); and many others. Check out distributors like Corel, Betacom, Autoskills and Visuaide. See Appendix G for addresses.

Spell Checkers

THE FRANKLIN SPELLING ACE The Franklin Spelling Ace is an easy-to-use portable speller and word list maker which helps with spelling, crossword puzzles and a variety of word games. It has a built-in lexicon of over 80,000 words, proper names and abbreviations. The manual used to boast that it uses nearly twice as many words as author Edgar Allan Poe. This hand-held spell checker is a great asset for literacy students, especially upper level students plagued by poor spelling. Punch in an incorrect word, and the Franklin gives a choice of correctly spelled words to choose from as a replacement. It is fallible, however. There are instances where it will not give you the word you are looking for, but nobody's perfect! (Least of all a machine.) The Franklin is available at Radio Shack stores as well as at electronic, department and office supply stores.

APPENDIX F
Digit Span Test

Digits Forward

Digits – Trial 1		**Digits – Trial 2**
Level 1	9-8-5	2-1-7
Level 2	5-7-3-1	1-4-7-2
Level 3	3-5-2-9-8	4-5-1-8-9
Level 4	6-7-3-5-8-2	9-5-3-8-2-1
Level 5	2-3-9-5-7-8-1	3-2-8-6-5-4-9
Level 6	1-5-3-8-6-7-9-2	5-7-4-8-2-3-9-1

Digits Backward

Digits – Trial 1		**Digits – Trial 2**
Level 1	4-6-8	7-3-9
Level 2	6-3-9-1	2-7-4
Level 3	5-3-8-2-6	9-7-1-8-6
Level 4	3-6-8-2-9-5	9-2-1-7-4-8-3
Level 5	5-3-6-2-9-7-1	1-5-7-3-8-9-4-2
Level 6	4-2-6-1-7-8-5-9	8-6-3-2-4-1-9-7-5

Instructions

~ Read level one *forward* digits, one trial at a time, at the rate of one word per second.

~ Do not repeat the digits, even if asked to do so.

~ Have the student repeat the numbers back to you.

~ Continue the same process, reading the numbers in the other levels.

~ When two failures occur at the same level, stop.

~ Now read the digits *backward* section, one trial a time, at the rate of one per second.

~ But first, say to the student, "This time, when I say the digits, you say them backwards. For example, if I say 7-9-2 you say 2-9-7."

~ When two failures occur at the same level, stop.

~ The average adult can repeat six digits forward and five digits backwards.

~ If an adult can repeat only four or fewer digits, it is very likely that he has problems with memory span, which means he may have difficulty registering and remembering spoken language as it goes by him at a normal rate.

~ A difference of more than two digits between the repetition of digits forward and digits backward (say six forward and three backward) also suggests some kind of difficulty in processing and understanding.

APPENDIX G
Useful Addresses

AHEAD (Association on Higher Education and Disability)

P.O. Box 21192
Columbus, Ohio 43221
Tel. (617) 287-3880

AUTOSKILL INTERNATIONAL INC.

301-331 Cooper Street
Ottawa, Ontario K2P 0G5
Tel. (613) 235-6740
Tel. 1-800-288-6754

BETACOM CORPORATION

450 Mathesen Blvd. East
Mississauga, Ontario L4Z 1R5
Tel. 1-800-353-1107

**THE ORDER CENTRE
COREL INC.**

P.O. Box 1036
Buffalo, NY 14240

THE IRLEN CENTRE

200 First Avenue
Ottawa, Ontario K1S 2G6
Tel. (613) 230-3995

**LEARNING ASSOCIATES
OF MONTREAL**

4203 Ste-Catherine Street West
Montreal, Quebec H3Z 1P6
Tel. (514) 989-9360

**NATIONAL LITERACY
SECRETARIAT**

25 Eddy Street, 11th Floor
Hull, Quebec K1A 0M3
Tel. (819) 953-5460

**THE OTTAWA LEARNING
CENTRE**

99 Rideau Street, 2nd Floor
Ottawa, Ontario K1N 9L8
Tel. (613) 239-2687

PEMBROOKE PUBLISHERS LTD.

538 Hood Road
Markham, Ontario L3R 3K9
Tel. 1-800-997-9807

**RECLAIM (The Reading Council
for Literacy Advance in
Montreal)**

4350 Ste-Catherine St. W.
Westmount, Quebec H3Z 1R3
Tel. (514) 369-7835

POOR RICHARD'S SOFTWARE

P.O. Box 1075
Litchfield, CT., USA 06759
Tel. (203) 567-4307

VISUAIDE

841 Jean-Paul Vincent
Longueuil, Quebec J4G 1E3
Tel. (450) 463-1717

VISUAL EDUCATION CENTRE

41 Horner Avenue, Unit 3
Etobicoke, Ontario M8Z 4X4
Tel. 1-800-668-0749

Some Internet Addresses

www.ldac-taac.ca/

This is the Web site of the Learning Disabilities Association of
Canada. They are dedicated to advancing the education,
employment, social development, legal rights and general well-
being of people with learning disabilities.

www.coe.uga.edu/ldcenter/homepage.html

This site belongs to the Learning Disabilities Center of the University
of Georgia. Its purpose is to promote student independence,
self-advocacy and success in an accessible university setting.

www.the-literacy-center.com/

This Web site belongs to The Literacy Center, which specializes
in helping individuals meet their literacy potential. The Literacy
Center specializes in speech recognition and literacy services
and products.

www.ldao.on.ca/

This site belongs to The Learning Disabilities Association of
Ontario, a charitable non-profit organization dedicated to
improving the lives of children, youth and adults with
learning disabilities.

www.rit.edu/~easi/pubs/ldnoelbw.htm

This is the Learning Disabilities Research and Training Center site.
The research and training is for and about adolescents and adults
with specific learning disabilities.

www.dyslexia.cyberus.ca/english/contents_e.htm
This is the site of the Canadian Dyslexia Association. Their mandate is to promote awareness of dyslexia, and develop and implement specialized methods, to improve quality of life of the estimated five million Canadians who have dyslexia.

www.learning-styles.com/
This site belongs to Learning Styles & Solutions, a full-service clinic for children and adults with learning disabilities. Services such as academic testing, psycho-educational evaluations, language training, occupational therapy, general academic support and organizational and study skills are offered on an individual basis.

www.rfbd.org
This web site contains over 80,000 recordings for the blind and dyslexic, on tape as well as other formats.

lbrinckerhoff@aol.com
Dr. Loring Brinckerhoff is a higher education learning disability consultant. His site provides visitors with information on a variety of learning disability aspects.

www.utoronto.ca/atrc
This is the University of Toronto's Web site for their Adaptive Technology Resource Center. Click on Web Resources for their 'Learning Disabilities Resources' section.

www.nald.ca
This is the Web site for the National Adult Literacy Database (NALD). This site includes links to a variety of Canadian literacy sites.

www.dyslexia.com
This British Web site contains useful links to computer resources.

www.knowledgetree.on.ca
Knowledge Tree Inc. is an importer/distributor of high quality educational software with dealers throughout Canada.

www.LDAAmerica.org

This site belongs to the Learning Disabilities Association of America. They work to advance the education and welfare of people with perceptual, conceptual or coordinative handicaps.

www.interdys.org/

This is the International Dyslexia Association web site. This association is a non-profit, scientific and educational organization dedicated to the study and treatment of dyslexia.

www.nldline.com/welcome.htm

This site provides information on NLD (Non-Verbal Learning Disability).

www.chadd.org/

CHADD is an organization that helps people who suffer from Attention Deficit Disorder.

www.novel.nifl.gov/nalld/nalldpub.htm

This site displays many newsletters related to Learning Disabilities.

APPENDIX H
Suggested Reading

Bringing Literacy Within Reach: Identifying and Teaching Adults with Learning Disabilities. Learning Disabilities Association of Canada. 1991.

Gardner, Howard, *Frames of Mind—The Theory of Multiple Intelligence.* Harvard University Press. Cambridge, MA. 1983.

Hallowell, Dr. David, *Driven to Distraction.* Pantheon Books. 1994.

Hampshire, Susan, *Susan's Story.* Sphere Books Ltd. New York. 1982.

Hayes, Marnell, *You Don't Outgrow It: Living with Learning Disabilities.* Academic Therapy Publications. Novaro, California. 1993.

Hornsby, Beve, *Overcoming Dyslexia.* Prentice-Hall. Toronto. 1986.

Johnson, Doris and Blalock, Jan. (eds.) *Adults With Learning Disabilities.* Grune and Stratton. Toronto. 1987.

Kelly, Kate and Ramundo, Peggy, *You Mean I'm Not Lazy, Stupid or Crazy?! A Self-Help Book for Adults with Attention Deficit Disorder.* Simon & Schuster.

Simpson, Eileen, *Reversals: A Personal Account of Victory Over Dyslexia.* Houghton.

Solden, Sari, *Women with Attention Deficit Disorder.* Underwood Books, Grass Valley, CA. 1995.

About the author

Ricki Goldstein studied education and special education at McGill University in Montreal. She has taught in regular, accelerated and special education classes in elementary schools, in Quebec and British Columbia.

Year 2000 marks her 20th year in literacy. Her experience in the field has been varied. She has taught literacy classes, developed curriculum materials, co-ordinated projects, conferences and programs and acted as a workshop leader. Currently Ricki is the Executive director of RECLAIM (Reading Council for Literacy Advance in Montreal).